Your Child Is Bright!
make the most of it

DR. BERNARD GREEN

ST. MARTIN'S PRESS • *New York*

Copyright © 1982 by Bernard Green
For information, write: St. Martin's Press,
175 Fifth Avenue, New York, N.Y. 10010
Manufactured in the United States of America

Library of Congress Cataloging in Publication Data

Green, Bernard, 1934–
Your child is bright!

1. Intellect. 2. Child rearing. I. Title.
BF431.G773   649'.1   81-16708
    ISBN 0-312-89771-5   AACR2

Design by George Laws
10 9 8 7 6 5 4 3 2 1
First Edition

This book is not intended to replace the services
of a physician. Any application of the
recommendations set forth in the following pages
is at the reader's discretion and sole risk.

Your Child Is
Bright!
make the most of it

Also by Bernard Green

GOODBYE, BLUES, BREAKING THE TRANQUILIZER HABIT THE NATURAL WAY

To my son, Tyler—my best teacher,
and to Judith, my wife,
whose creative spark
made it all begin.

ACKNOWLEDGMENTS

To all who helped—Dominick Abel, Ted Schwarz,
Judith Carrington, Katharine Homer Fryer
and the staff of the Fryer Research Center,
Abram Hoffer, Linus Pauling, Tom Dunne,
Ashton Applewhite, Adelle Davis, and Pir Vilayat Khan.

CONTENTS

INTRODUCTION • page xi

CHAPTER 1 • page 1
What Kind of Kid Have I Really Got?

CHAPTER 2 • page 7
Just What Is Normal, Anyway?

CHAPTER 3 • page 33
Nutrition Makes the Mind Go Round

CHAPTER 4 • page 45
Mind Games Are as Much Fun as Toy Games

CHAPTER 5 • page 71
Pressing Your Child's Magic Button

CHAPTER 6 • page 87
*It's Better to Give than to Receive,
but Try to Tell a Two-year-old*

CHAPTER 7 • page 99
*Communicating with Your Child,
or How to Rap with a Toddler to a Teen*

CHAPTER 8 • page 133
Bedtime Manners to Sleep By

CHAPTER 9 • page 147
Coping with Problems

CHAPTER 10 • page 163
Conclusion

APPENDIX • page 165

BIBLIOGRAPHY • page 169

INDEX • page 171

INTRODUCTION

The developed mind of a child is a parent's gift of love to the world. That precious mind used to its capabilities results in a fulfilled adult who excels in areas of his or her abilities.

The potential for greatness in converting intelligence into achievement exists within everyone, but too frequently is only partially developed. Many children are considered just "average" throughout their growing years because their exceptional qualities have not been reached. These may be beneath the surface, hidden from the schoolteachers and other professionals to whom we assign the task of developing our children. However, you, the parent, can discover and develop the exceptional qualities within your child.

For more than twenty years I have worked as a therapist in the United States and around the world. At first my practice involved troubled children and their families. Then I began to realize that one of the most overlooked areas of human development was the normal child in a good home, a child like yours. Parents want to know how they can help their children to be the best of which they are capable. Because I had no answers, I decided to devote some of my work to understanding the components that would help to bring forth exceptional qualities.

During the past several years I have worked with thousands of children and their parents, as well as with my own children. In this time, based on the latest research in nutrition, psychology, and physiology, I have explored new and exciting ways to challenge a child to achieve the best. One important insight that was reaffirmed over and over again is that there is *no* teacher who has the very special communication ability with a child that the parent does.

The plan contained within this book is the result of my research. Basically it is a four-part approach to child raising which is fun, easy to do, and can be handled by any parent, no matter how much or how little time you might have each week for intense involvement with your child.

The first part of the plan bears on nutrition. Children seem able to eat nearly anything and still thrive. They delight in soft drinks, candy, ice cream, and all kinds of fast food, all of which parents know are not good for them, yet the children grow tall, strong, and healthy. However, improper nutrition takes its toll in a child's inability to concentrate, hyperactivity, unusual fatigue, and a general behavior and attitude pattern that parents may have come to accept as normal.

The nutrition information shows how certain foods and vitamins affect your child. For example, it shows how choline, one of the B-complex vitamins, ensures that the nerve synapses, which affect physical and mental reaction time, will be healthy. Vitamin C and B-complex all affect a child's emotional state and the ability to handle stress. Certain vitamins, such as B-3 in the form of niacinamide, act as a natural tranquilizer. Dolomite, a natural combination of calcium and magnesium, can help a child with sleep problems to rest at night, ensuring mental freshness in the morning.

The chapter shows what food does, how processed "junk" food needs missing nutrients in order to be metabolized, and how even a slight change in your child's eating habits can make a major difference in achieving exceptional qualities. Details of what each vitamin does for the mental and physical development of your child is also included.

Children need to learn to concentrate both for relaxation and learning. The longer a child's attention span, the faster he or she will develop exceptional qualities. Thus the second part of my program involves fantasy games and meditation techniques. You will learn to help your child play games which teach concentration, relaxation, and positive thinking.

The games have a second value. They allow you to interact with your child in a way that is both intellectually stimulating and emotionally strengthening. Since you and your spouse both are likely to hold jobs, it is important that the limited time you are able to spend with your child be productive for you all.

The games, like the other sections of this book, are grouped according to the age of your child. The changes are minor, each game increasing in sophistication, though with the same developmental results. I have used the different games with infants through teenagers, always successfully.

Games also will help your child to understand others. A child who has difficulty in school or in getting along with other children can be helped through the fantasy games you will learn. Your child will gain peace of mind while you come to understand some of the underlying emotional forces in his or her life. You will learn how to have a dialogue which reveals your child's true feelings, then further games which will help your child to gain better self-understanding in order to handle the problems.

Talking out problems and communicating with your child are presented to help you to advance your child's thinking to the point where he or she can handle sophisticated concepts. Each level of childhood has its limits in the way a child can perceive the world around. You will come to understand how each age group differs in its level of understanding; thus you need new ways to communicate feelings and ideas so your child will always understand. Too frequently parents become frustrated when they can't seem to communicate what, to them, are simple concepts. By learning how a child thinks at different ages, it is possible to communicate extremely complex ideas and to have your child understand them fully. This part of the program will help your child to develop intellectual superiority compared with others of the same age.

The final portion of the plan involves exercise and rest. A child needs physical outdoor activity every day in order to be able to relax and concentrate. The sun supplies a natural tranquilizer in the form of vitamin D to help them absorb calcium and maintain hormonal balance. Your child should be out in the natural light for at least thirty minutes each day, in order for this process to work. With this natural calmative, your child will have an easier time functioning in all other endeavors. Without it, your child may become hyperactive, depressed, be unable to concentrate.

That each child gets satisfying and adequate rest is important for achieving peak performance. Yet children often have sleep problems.

The section on sleep enables you to learn what is normal and how to help your child sleep better when emotions and other factors may hinder normal rest.

Finally the book tells you how to cope with problems. The plan—nutrition, exercise, fantasy games, communication, and rest—can help every parent to raise an exceptional child. Starting this plan at birth and using it throughout childhood should result in the maximum development of your child's mind, body, and emotional stability. However, if you have an older child, you may find that some of your child's past experiences have created minor barriers to learning. The last chapter will discuss what to do if your child has one of the common learning and/or personal growth difficulties. The chapter shows you how to spot them and deal with them so that your child can go forward and achieve to the limits of his or her abilities.

The plan sounds simple in concept and implementation because it has taken me over twenty years of working with children and adults to develop and refine it. Basically, there are just four steps to follow, yet by following the program outlined, you will find you can unleash those exceptional qualities which might otherwise remain hidden for all of your child's life.

1

What Kind of Kid Have I Really Got?

When four-year-old Michael Stone unplugged the television set, took a box of Tinker Toys, and proceeded to use the various parts to create the most sophisticated digital computer ever invented, his parents knew their child was exceptional. When seven-year-old Leslie Meyer sat down at the family's typewriter and proceeded to write a novel which spent sixteen weeks on the *New York Times*' best-seller list, her parents realized she was unusually advanced. When six-year-old Jamie Trimble took a box of crayons and a piece of paper, then produced a work of art favorably compared with the Old Masters and now hanging in the Metropolitan Museum of Art, his parents also recognized the genius in their child. Yet when your small child spills a glass of milk for the fourth time in the same meal, you can not help but wonder if the child is truly realizing his or her full potential.

The most average child has latent exceptional qualities, which, if tapped, reveal creative abilities. These qualities take various forms. Some children have exceptional visual capacity, others gifts for reason and logic, others mechanical aptitude, others verbal dexterity. Yet with all this potential, the superior qualities frequently go unrecognized. Children who are stimulated only by television, preschool facilities which are frequently little more than baby-sitting services, and schools whose teachers may fear innovative methods, may never realize these special gifts.

I want to show you how to evaluate your child, understand his or her current development, then work with your child to bring forth his or her hidden potential.

There are several myths about child development. The most prominent is that a parent knows nothing about creativity and that only trained teachers can develop this ability.

This is not the case. You are the best teacher your child can have. If you are the mother, you have a mental, physical, and spiritual symbiotic attachment with your child from the moment of conception to your baby's first cry. If you are the father, you watch the fetus grow within your wife. The emotional environment you create through your relationship with her and your attitude toward the impending birth can affect your unborn child.

From birth your child will love you both, trust you both, and rely on you for survival and growth. Your child respects what you have to say, thinking you are omniscient.

You may wonder if you are up to this awesome job. There are several reasons why you are. You are an adult with the accumulated wisdom and understanding of many years. If you can impart your adult knowledge, your child will have wisdom beyond his or her years—and this becomes the basis for learning upon which his or her life is built.

You are also the best teacher because your young child will listen to you. A professional teacher will not enter your child's life for several years, and even then the teacher's attention must be shared with twenty or thirty others. It will be several weeks or months into the school year before the teacher understands your child and earns his or her trust. Only when this communication is established can the teacher be an effective motivator. Sometimes this never happens, or sometimes it occurs so late in the school year that the child is ready to move to another grade and another teacher.

From the moment your baby first learns to explore the world, you can work with your child, using the methods in this book. By the time your child first encounters the school system, he or she will have developed the individuality that will single out your child as being exceptional.

"But even if what you say is true, I don't have all that much time. I work for a living and can't quit my job to be a teacher twenty-four hours a day," you may say to yourself.

It is the *quality* not the quantity of time you spend with your child which determines the growth of creative abilities. It is your understanding of the process of your child's mental growth, of the role you can play that is the determinant. This will be reflected in the quality of the time you spend together, whether reading a book, taking a walk, or building block structures together.

For many centuries, parents felt themselves capable of raising children without outside specialized help. Their successes were numerous. Think of the numerous doctors, scientists, humanitarians, and world leaders who walked the earth for centuries before anyone ever heard of Sigmund Freud and the field of psychoanalysis. Their parents were not geniuses, but people just like you and me. They recognized that it was within their power and ability to help their children achieve their fullest potential and there were no popular psychology magazines to make them feel otherwise.

Today, parents are intimidated by the complex jargon that comes from classical psychoanalysis. They are aware that mood-altering drugs are widely administered for even the mildest emotional upsets or behavioral deviations. Instead of looking to themselves, talking to their own families, or to their peers about their confusions, they are inclined to look for an outside "fix," an expert, a medication. They forget that no one will ever really know their child as they do. We parents are being brainwashed by some child psychiatrists into fearing to love, fearing to discipline, fearing to trust our instincts and knowledge when raising children we know best.

Even extreme activity, often a sign of intense curiosity which needs to be nurtured and channeled in positive directions, can be stifled by the so-called "experts." One community in New Jersey began using the pharmaceutical Ritalin on a broad basis to reduce the extreme activity of children in the schoolrooms. "Specialists" in child behavior said the normal activity represented a physical problem. Ritalin was created to treat the disturbance—medically called hyperactivity—so the parents were told to get their doctors to give their children the drug. The result was that the children were quiet, drugged, near-zombies who were no longer active, or intensely curious and no longer a challenge to teachers. Sadly, the drug was actually misused when prescribed toward this end, a problem with the school system, not the manufacturer. What was needed were better teachers who knew how to channel the children's attention and normal activities. Thus hundreds suffered because a school board had bowed to the pressures of experts.

It is unfortunate but true that more imaginative children who do not exactly follow the beaten path can represent a problem to both parents and teachers. Suppression of this originality does not bring out the creativity that this book is all about. What's easiest for parents and teachers isn't always the mode that instills free thinking and breakthrough ideas in your child's later life.

The fact is that your child does not need pharmaceuticals to control his or her behavior. The way to a creative child is simple and within your abilities. It takes love, no more time than you would otherwise spend, and neither drugs nor "expert" counsel. This book shows you how to do it.

You may wonder "What will happen when my child enters school? What if my child is ahead of the others? Will boredom be a problem?"

Children have never entered school at the same developmental level. One child races through a math course and will be working on more advanced problems. Another child picks up reading so quickly that she is considerably ahead of the rest of the class. A third child might be average in reading and math while excelling in art. Your early work with your child will help him find his level. School for your child is only one part of his education. The most important part, at this early age is with you.

Working at home with your child is one of the most satisfying and important aspects of being a parent. There are various ways to stimulate his or her natural curiosity. Some examples for three- to six-year-olds are:

1. Start a story and let him or her finish it.
2. Join with puzzles, but you never put the piece in the right

place. Talk to him or her about what shape or color would fit in where.
3. Read a story and see if the child can repeat details of the plot. Point to an illustration and see if he knows what happened on that page. See if the child's attention can be held even if he doesn't see the picture.
4. With drawing play "copy cat." Make a design or picture and have them copy it. In kind, let them make a design or picture for you to copy. You can write out numbers and letters and complicated forms with dots and dashes for your child to complete.
5. When you go on a trip with your child let him keep a journal. Write down his version of what he did and let him illustrate the description.
6. With math and counting, get a big pad of poster paper or a blackboard and work with simple addition and subtraction and play with making numbers.

In the next chapter, a series of planned observations can be used to evaluate the growth of your child. We will then show you how to enhance your child's exceptional qualities which will amaze you. No matter what expectations you may have in the present, you will find by the end of this book, that the results will be greater than any you could have imagined. Most important is that *you* will have created that opportunity for your child.

2

Just What Is Normal, Anyway?

Childhood growth comes in stages and not every child grows in the same way or at the same rate. One child might have certain physical coordination at the age of two that a second child, the same age, will not develop for several months more. A third child might have the ability to perceive shapes of certain types when she is three while her best friend will be nearly four before she achieves this skill. This is all normal and, just because I am listing the approximate differences with each age, do not consider my statements to be hard-and-fast rules. They are guidelines to give you a broad understanding of development.

Throughout this chapter are a number of tests for you to take; they are nothing more than controlled observations of your child's normal activities. After you have taken the tests compare them with the guidelines. The results are to help direct your thinking as you start to aid in the intellectual growth of your child.

A TEST FOR THE PARENTS OF ONE-YEAR-OLDS
(If your child is older, skip ahead to the appropriate test.)
(Score 10 points for A, 5 *for* B, *and* 0 *for* C)

1. You smile at your child. Does your child
    A. Smile back
    B. Ignore you
    C. Start to cry

2. When you enter his or her room, does your child
    A. Look up expectantly
    B. Continue what he's doing
    C. Pretend he's asleep
3. Does your child respond to the game of "bye-bye"
    A. Usually
    B. Sometimes
    C. Never
4. When your child is exposed to music, does he or she
    A. Listen to and enjoy that music
    B. Ignore the music
    C. Shut off the radio
5. Does your child love to have an audience
    A. Yes
    B. Sometimes
    C. No
6. Does your child love to use two or more words in addition to "mama" and "dada" or your child's equivalent terms for you and your spouse
    A. Yes
    B. Sometimes
    C. Never
7. Does your child cooperate when being dressed
    A. Yes
    B. Sometimes
    C. Never
8. Can your child
    A. Walk a few steps alone
    B. Walk with one hand held
    C. Only crawl

The closer your child comes to achieving 80 points, the greater the exceptional qualities he or she has already developed for this age. Our knowledge of early infancy is limited. The baby is unresponsive in many ways simply because he or she is still in a primitive stage of development. The infant frequently falls into a shallow sleep. For example, a four-week-old infant has the ability to open his or her eyes widely, breathe more regularly, and sleep better.

Some individual preference will be shown by the four-week-old. The way he or she lies on one side when awake will show that one position is more desirable. The infant will also react by crying when in pain or denied something.

By sixteen weeks, an infant has greatly developed his motor skills.

The sixteen-week-old infant wants to be held with greater frequency. He is curious about the world which he likes to see by being propped erect for short periods. The child's motor skills are better coordinated and he or she can follow a moving object with the eyes and head. The infant is responsive to attention, cooing, chuckling, and general activity around him.

At twenty-eight weeks of age, she is ready to sit up. The child likes to handle objects with her crude grasp. The child brings everything to her mouth, including her feet.

The twenty-eight-week-old child is intrigued by each newly acquired skill. The child can pass an object from hand to hand, fascinating himself for long periods. The child likes to have the parents talk and responds to their voices.

The child of twenty-eight weeks understands the absence of parents and will cry when mother leaves, then become frustrated when she fails to return on demand. He fears abandonment. The frustrations at this age are many.

In between the periods mentioned, your child has times when she seems to be regressing slightly. Nothing quite works and the child is unable to maintain equilibrium at tasks which seemingly have been accomplished before. One problem period is at twenty weeks. Another is at around thirty-two weeks. The older the child becomes, the greater his or her awareness of what is happening and the lag between what is permissible and what is desirable. The frustration expresses itself in what seems to the parent to be senseless crying. The diapers are not wet, the child is neither hungry nor thirsty, and nothing seems to stop the tears. It is all a sense of helpless rage.

The one-year-old child usually has excellent mobility. Probably you have been both amused and frustrated as he or she barrels through the living room, moving about the furniture, pulling things down from tables. Your child likes people and delights in having an audience. This is the earliest that a child develops self-confidence and friendliness.

At one year, your baby likes peek-a-boo, chase, and other games. Your baby is determined to be independent, and will insist upon standing when being fed and will manipulate the spoon for his or her self. This is a messy time, though the greater the independence you encourage, the faster the child will develop. One year is not too soon to begin challenging your baby to reach beyond what might, at first, appear to be his or her limits.

Some parents and many child development "experts" think that the baby in the six-month to one-year age group cannot develop exceptional qualities because the physical development is primitive and the attention span is limited. However, even if you won't be able to notice the development for six months to a year, it is occurring.

The most important way to begin stimulating development of your six-month to one-year-old child is through sensory stimulation. Talk with your child, treating him or her as a tiny person, not as an undeveloped creature without comprehension. Babies play language games with sound. Their babble is purposeful, both as entertainment and as a way of learning to put sounds together for effective communication. A baby has the capacity to imitate every kind of human speech heard anywhere in the world—from the "click" talk of a primitive African tribe to the complex tongue of an Asian mountain village to the language you are reading. This ability, coupled with an instinctive desire to communicate, makes the baby gradually refine the sounds until the speech of his or her parents can be imitated.

Some parents find this babble so appealing (kitchy koo, iddy biddy baby poo, and so on) that they imitate the problems the child is having. The parents call it "talking baby talk," never realizing that the child is trying to imitate full adult language. If you talk "baby talk" you hinder your child's verbal development. When you ignore the language failings, which are often adorably humorous, and continue to speak as you would to a fellow adult, your child begins to fine-tune his ear. Your baby develops verbal ability which, by the time the child is two, will be exceptional when compared with other children. Usually such a child speaks in full sentences while others are just stringing three or four words together, getting the point across but showing almost no mastery of the language.

How should you talk to your child? There are two ways: (1) talking generally and (2) naming specific objects. Initially, share with your infant whatever the two of you happen to encounter. This can start at six months. For example, I saw the mother of a newborn in a grocery store. Most of the time the baby slept, but when he was awake, I watched the mother talk with him. "Do you think this bunch of carrots will please your father? I know they're a little soft, but they do seem to be the best ones here." The baby gurgled slightly, not really aware of anything the mother was saying. However, she continued on, "I suppose you're right. We'll buy something else for the salad. If we don't use all these up, they'll probably spoil and that's just a waste of money."

The baby drifted back to sleep. Then, later in the store, when he stirred awake again, she discussed canned goods, labels, and prices with him. Of course she was really talking to herself more than the baby, since she knew the child would not understand her words. That was all right; she was letting the baby hear the English language spoken by an adult. During the weeks to come, the baby would use her words for the refinement of sound. Her actions were laying the foundation for exceptional verbal skills. Had she not respected her baby, even during this period of truly limited capacity, his growth would have been correspondingly restricted.

Between ages six months to one year, you should start being specific with your baby. Your child's attention span may be only a few seconds but this is long enough to provide meaningful language training. Each time you do anything, show the baby what it is and say the name. Say "bottle" when you show him or her the bottle. Say "diaper" when appropriate. Identify yourself, your spouse, other family members, pets, items in the house. Doing this repeatedly builds a large vocabulary at an early age. This seems simple but parents often do not do it.

The specifying of objects will speed a child's language development. Remember: young children understand more than they articulate.

Continue talking with your baby as you did when he or she was little more than a newborn. The conversation allows the baby to begin stringing the new words together at an earlier age. This combination of stimuli—conversation and object specifying—is what will cause your child, at around age two, to sound more sophisticated than other children the same age. Your child will have exceptional language skills which will be utilized throughout life.

The other kinds of creative stimulation you can provide at this age are visual and auditory. Play music for your child. It can be classical, rock, country-western, easy listening, or anything else. You might even try a little of each, varying the music throughout the day. This can be when the baby is awake or even as quiet background when your baby is sleeping. The musical awareness slowly builds an enjoyment which, when your child is somewhat older, will lead to an attempt to sing or play an instrument. This also helps develop motor skills and mathematical ability with a resulting sense of self-worth and accomplishment.

The visual stimulation comes from murals, mobiles, pictures, toys, and other items placed in, around, and above your baby's bed. These should be colorful, differently shaped, and rotated for variety. It is not important how much your baby can perceive during these first few months of life. What matters is that the stimulation is present.

Always keep in mind that a baby is in many ways no different from an adult. If the baby sees the same sights day after day, he or she will become bored. Your baby will mentally turn off the surroundings, much as you stop looking at the familiar in the room. The difference is that you will find new ways for stimulation and your baby cannot. Your baby, unable to move about, is dependent upon the changes in visual environment which you provide. If you do not regularly vary these decorations, your baby will mentally withdraw.

I mentioned earlier that every child develops uniquely, even though there are patterns which exist when large numbers of children are studied as a group. One child has a parent who talks with her and is speaking full sentences at age two. Another child has a parent who does the same thing, yet her verbal skills are not as developed. Yet both are likely to be exceptional. Both parents are helping their children reach full potential.

Albert Einstein is an example of a child who did not follow the "normal" pattern. Einstein's speech was extremely limited until well past age three, even though other children the same age were talking animatedly. He flunked mathematics in elementary school because he saw the flaws in current knowledge and stopped trying to compete. Yet he unlocked the secrets of the universe. By keeping in mind this individuality of mental, physical, emotional, and spiritual growth, you will not be discouraged by arbitrary standards. The methods *do* work. They help your child or children achieve their true potential. How fast your child develops in relation to others is not important.

A TEST FOR THE PARENTS OF TWO-YEAR-OLDS

(Score 10 points for A, 5 for B, and 0 for C)

1. When your two-year-old at bedtime says, "Just one more kiss," do you
   A. Firmly give him one more kiss, explain that this is really goodnight, and that you'll see him in the morning
   B. Kiss her yet again and plead with her to go to bed
   C. Tell him to shut up and go to bed with an angry voice
2. If your two-year-old has smeared his stools on the wall do you
   A. Explain why this is an awful thing to do and tell him never to do it again
   B. Start spanking him
   C. Start cleaning it up and say nothing
3. If your two-year-old is sucking her thumb do you
   A. Explain why she shouldn't do this
   B. Ignore it, realizing it is age appropriate and will be a passing habit
   C. Spank
4. You say, "Come here"; your two-year-old ignores you. Do you
   A. Remain calm, get through his resistance by getting him to

focus and explain why it is important for him to come to you
   B. Ignore
   C. Scream at him to come here
5. Father comes home from work, offers to put the two-year-old to bed. Son or daughter says, "No, I want Mommy, not you!" Does he
   A. Realize that this is age-appropriate behavior and let Mommy put the child to bed without feeling neglected
   B. Put the child to bed anyway ignoring and coping with the objection
   C. Take it very personally and enter into a fight
6. Your two-year-old is fighting with his or her four-year-old sister. Do you
   A. Stay out of it
   B. Side with your younger because he is smaller
   C. Scream at both of them

The two-year-old is becoming socially mature, no longer continually wrapped up in "me." The two-year-old does not get instantly frustrated, but has the patience to wait a minute or two. A child of this age is more likely to share with other children.

I know that most people speak with exhaustion of the "terrible twos." They really mean that the experience of having a child who is two is one in which the child becomes rigid and inflexible. Waiting for gratification is unthinkable. He or she wants instant satisfaction of every demand. The idea that anything might deviate from expectations is unthinkable to a two-year-old.

The two-year-old child has violent emotions and little ability to stick with any decision. One minute he insists upon one activity, the next minute he may refuse to engage in it. At the same time, there is a rigidity which makes it necessary to read him four bedtime stories on Monday, the same four on Tuesday, the same four on Wednesday until, by the end of the week, you, the parent, are ready to scream.

Fortunately the approximately six months of total confusion during the second year ends quickly. The three-year-old actually knows how to say "yes" in contrast to his former determination to shout "no, no, no" to almost everything. The ritualistic way in which the two-year-old repeats activities ends quickly. The three-year-old is flexible, likes people, and can adjust to changes.

A TEST FOR THE PARENTS OF THREE-YEAR-OLDS

(Score 10 points for A, 5 for B, and 0 for C)

1. Your child is playing with another child in the playground. This second child is accidentally hurt. Does your child
   A. Help the second child or try to get help for that child
   B. Ignore the second child's injury, perhaps continuing to play
   C. Run away
2. This question relates to your child's attempts at art work. When your child has a pen, pencil, crayons, or other drawing device, he or she will scribble on the paper. Take a look at the scribbling.
   A. Is the scribbling meant to be a specific part of an object your child is trying to draw? Your child might be trying to draw the car in the garage of your house, the head of a boy, or some other specific object
   B. The scribblings are meant to have a purpose ("I'm drawing my best friend, Johnny" or "This is you and Daddy, Mommy" or "This is our apartment")
   C. The scribbling is angry, violent, lacking in any sort of visual harmony or purpose

(*Note:* Scribbles can be visually harmonious if your child has developed an inner harmony and an exceptional understanding of the world around. The scribbles may not make a great deal of sense, but the scribbles made with angry violence are quite obviously different from those which are attempts to represent specific people or objects.)

3. When your child listens to music, does he or she

A. Show a total awareness of the music by becoming truly absorbed? The child may nod his or her head in rhythm, perhaps tapping or clapping to the beat
   B. The child is obviously aware of the music but continues doing whatever activity he or she was enjoying before the music started. The child's awareness will be much like an office worker listening to recorded background music. The person knows it is there but does not really stop to absorb it all
   C. Your child ignores the music entirely
4. Your child has been exposed to poetry, simple rhymes, and similar intellectual stimulation in these three years of life. Without your supplying words and clues, does your child
   A. Know a few rhymes which he or she can recite
   B. Only occasionally tell rhymes, often when encouraged by a friend or parent, but not on any regular basis
   C. Never vocalize rhymes and may not have learned any
5. When it comes to social behavior, your child
   A. Likes to make new friends and will actively seek others when given the opportunity
   B. Shows an awareness of others and a degree of curiosity. However, shyness prevents any aggressiveness
   C. Ignores people, avoiding them entirely instead of just shyly observing from what is perceived as a safe distance
6. Your child is eating some favorite food. You ask for a bite of what he or she is obviously enjoying. Does your child
   A. Willingly let you take a bite of the food that is giving him or her pleasure
   B. Begrudgingly give you a small amount, often just a crumb or a tiny bite which you can take only under close scrutiny
   C. Eat it quickly, perhaps taking it away before you can get near it

(*Note:* This is a test of sharing, just as the art test is one relating to harmony. Thus it is a test of his or her willingness to share the experience of pleasure rather than thinking of only his personal enjoyment.)

7. When you give your child specific directions concerning what you expect your child to do
   A. He or she does what you asked because your child likes to please
   B. He or she sometimes does what is requested but not always
   C. Your child never does what is requested, often doing the opposite
8. Does your child say "I love you" to you
   A. Yes, fairly regularly
   B. Once in a while
   C. Never

The three-year-old is excited by language. Your child of this age mimics your speech, is delighted with new words as though they were almost magical in their powers to influence behavior.

At three and a half, a child develops a better understanding of body and mind, as well as their limitations. The child wants to do something and usually can. The child no longer insists upon tackling an obviously impossible task.

At three and a half, a child may show some signs of emotional insecurity, such as stuttering. A child will cry, whine, bite his nails, pick his nose, blink his eyes, suck his thumb, and masturbate. Your child may frequently need reassurance that you love him. Your child may insist upon being the center of attention. Rivalry among brothers and sisters can be great. He or she wants a roomful of people to be constantly aware of her every activity.

When a child reaches four, she rebels against socially acceptable behavior. Such a child will attempt every "bad" thing he can do. This is the time of kicking, biting, stone throwing, breaking of objects, and even running away to "punish" you.

Four-year-olds delight in shocking people with their language. They usually find humor in words relating to bathroom functions.

Every swear word he or she hears will be adopted, usually in front of the one person guaranteed to cause embarrassment.

Many four-year-olds live in a world where fantasy and reality blend. There are no limits to the imagination. What sounds like a lie might be the child's perception of the truth. This is a marvelous age to challenge your child's imagination and creativity.

By the time six months have passed, the four-and-a-half-year-old is seeing life more realistically. The child's imagination is active but he knows the difference between fantasy and reality.

A TEST FOR THE PARENTS OF FOUR-YEAR-OLDS

(Score 10 points for A, 5 for B, and 0 for C)

1. Your four-year-old breaks your favorite vase. Do you
    A. Ask him why he did that? Tell him firmly and calmly that you are very annoyed and hurt and must remove him from the scene to his bedroom to think about his behavior
    B. Scream at him
    C. Hit him
2. Your four-year-old says a four-letter word in front of your friends. Do you
    A. Tell him that you never want him to use those words and send him to his bedroom to think about his behavior
    B. Wash his mouth out with soap
    C. Hit him
3. If he defies your commands, do you
    A. Explain in a calm and loving way why he has to do what you ask
    B. Scream at him to do so
    C. Hit him
4. He swaggers like Bogart or Kojak, boasts, and defies you. Do you
    A. Ignore this realizing it is age appropriate
    B. Tell him to stop
    C. Chastise him

5. He runs across the street. Do you
   A. Graphically describe how he could kill himself
   B. Scream "Never again cross the street without me"
   C. Chastise him

Firmness is needed in dealing with a four-year-old. The four-year-old behavior is "out-of-bounds" as Ilg and Bates say in *Child Behavior:* "Keep in mind that behaving in an out-of-bounds manner is not only an almost inevitable but a probably quite necessary part of development."

In my work with children, I have found that four-and-a-half-year-olds take literally what they see on television. This can create serious problems if a child's viewing is not controlled. One woman told me she thought her child was lying to her about seeing someone killed. "I just saw the woman next door killed," said the four-and-a-half-year-old daughter. "I got so mad at her," said the mother. "I told her she was telling lies again. I told her she had to tell the truth, especially about something so bad as that."

I decided to talk with the little girl to understand what was happening. "I just saw the woman next door being killed," the girl repeated.

"That's terrible, Joan. Where did you see it?" I asked. The little girl may have had no conception of death but she was obviously upset by the bad act that she had seen.

"My mommy has a little box in her room on the shelf, and if you look at the box, you can see the people next door. I looked at the box and I saw the people next door, and then I saw the woman next door being killed."

Joan wasn't telling a lie. She had no concept of television. She had come to the conclusion that the box was, in essence, a window through to the next apartment. Anything she saw was very real, even though the more sophisticated understanding of her parents made them not recognize what was happening.

This situation is not unusual for a child of that age. She was attempting to sort out the difference between fantasy and reality. Joan came to understand the "pretend" aspect of the television show, yet remained frightened of the "bogeyman" who was a very real threat to her.

Another example of how children's fantasies and reality blend is seen in Tim and his imaginary friend, No-no.

Tim was a blond, blue-eyed four-year-old who said a defiant "no" to everybody. He was nervous and irritable. One day, when his parents asked why he said "no" all the time, he replied, "because No-no tells me to."

"Who is No-no?"

"No-no lives in my room, sleeps in my bed, and comes to school with me."

No-no was an imaginary companion who told Tim not to eat.

The parents brought Tim to see me and I arranged for a hair analysis test, which shows what minerals are lacking. The results revealed a dire lack of calcium, magnesium, and zinc, which would cause irritability and inability to concentrate. These symptoms, which Tim's kindergarten teachers complained of, his parents had resigned themselves to as part of Tim's personality. They had a "difficult" child who projected these traits onto his imaginary friend, No-no.

No-no wasn't the problem, nor the projections; Tim's biochemistry was. I put him on a no-sugar, no-white flour, high protein diet, with daily supplements of calcium, magnesium, zinc, vitamin C, vitamin B^{100} complex, niacinamide, vitamin B^6, and pantothenic acid, and within two weeks, his teacher noted a "dramatic improvement in his ability to concentrate and focus."

Tim became a charming, sociable four-year-old, who stopped saying "no" to everything. He was friendly, cooperative, happy, and slept better. Before the vitamin regimen he refused to go to bed, fell asleep when exhausted, and got up in the middle of the night. Now he willingly went to bed and slept through the night.

Because he got on better with the other children, he had more friends and liked himself more.

What happened to No-no? Well, he is still around, but Tim reports that "No-no only says 'no' when he should," which, by the way, is usually appropriate.

Children of this age are able to sustain interest in ideas and facts. If you read your children a book about the Wright brothers, they want to continue talking about flying after you are done.

If you read "Little Red Riding Hood" to your child at bedtime, he will still be in the forest the next morning and want to know all about the big bad wolf!

Drawings become more complex and three-dimensional at four and a half. A child may draw the head of a man on the front of a piece of paper, then ask you if the paper can be turned over so the back of the head can be drawn.

A TEST FOR THE PARENTS OF FIVE- AND SIX-YEAR-OLDS

(Score 10 points for A, 5 for B, and 0 for C)

(*Note:* With all these tests, the closer to 80 your observations let you score, the greater the existing exceptional qualities of your child.)

1. Does your five-year-old child
   A. Want to be a "good" boy or a "good" girl
   B. Rebel most of the time
   C. Act in a perverse manner, not just rebelling but insisting upon acting in the opposite manner of what you want
2. Observe the artistic quality of your child when engaged in drawing. Does your five-year-old
   A. Produce human figures with some degree of accuracy but have trouble with abstract work
   B. Produce what are groups of harmonious scribbles using paint, pencils, crayons, etc.
   C. Produce scribblings without visual harmony or obvious purpose other than to fill the paper
3. Does your five-year-old have the mathematical skills to
   A. Count ten objects correctly
   B. Count five objects correctly
   C. Doesn't count at all

4. Does your five-year-old understand money by being able to
   A. Name a penny, a nickel, and a dime, correctly identifying each object
   B. Name and identify just a single coin
   C. Not be able to name any of these objects
5. Does your five-year-old understand guidance by
   A. Being able to follow specific directions
   B. Occasionally but not always utilizing the directions
   C. Rebelling at any sort of directions
6. When there is music in your home, does your five-year-old
   A. Like music, perhaps dancing to the music being played
   B. Ignore music
   C. Turn off the music, being hostile to having it on the radio or stereo
7. When it comes to interpersonal relationships, does your five-year-old
   A. Thrive on praise
   B. Not believe you are sincere when you give him or her praise
   C. Deliberately set up situations where he will be scolded instead of praised
8. When it comes to activities, is your five- to six-year-old content to
   A. Stay near home but usually prefers to be with other children. The child does not seek out a parent's company
   B. Stay near home, enjoying being with mother
   C. Be alone, withdrawn and not particularly responsive to others

The five-year-old child is quite secure, capable, and likable. He enjoys being taught new activities and expanding his abilities.

For the five-year-old child, the mother is the center of his world and he likes to be always near her, do things with and for her, and even obey her commands.

Gone is the out-of-bounds exuberance of the four-year-old. Their uncertainties subside. They like to be instructed and because they want parental approval, usually succeed in being a "good" child.

At six, the rhythms of childhood are expressed in periods of contentment, joy; and perfecting of skills followed by times of emotionalism, awkwardness, and contrariness. At six and a half comes the return of controls.

The seven-year-old child is easier to live with than he was a few months earlier. There is a sense of direction, a longer attention span, and a more relaxed attitude toward life.

The seven-year-old is not particularly social or aggressive. He or she likes to be alone watching television, playing, listening to the radio, and reading. The child watches others, trying to understand the world and his or her relationships within it.

There is an unquenchable drive to learn and achieve at seven, a drive that is not tempered with an understanding of personal limitations. The child will be active for hours, then suddenly become exhausted.

A mild paranoia is the normal way for many seven-year-olds. Teachers are against them, the other children pick on them, their parents don't understand them. One of my patients was a seven-year-old who insisted that he was adopted because he felt that nobody in the family loved him. This wasn't the case but he fantasized to such an extreme that he decided it was true and that the reason was that he was not the natural child. His situation was slightly extreme but not at all unusual. Most children of this age are slightly sad and dissatisfied, conditions parents regret, but cannot do very much to change.

When a child is in his or her eighth year, a mild aggressiveness replaces the tendency to withdraw. An eight-year-old can go anywhere, do anything, and meet anybody, or at least thinks she can. The world holds great excitement and great trauma. When failure hits, the tears and self-discouragement are exaggerated way out of proportion.

A TEST FOR THE PARENTS OF SEVEN- TO EIGHT-YEAR-OLDS

(Score 10 points for A, 5 for B, and 0 for C)

1. Your seven-year-old seems morose, mopey, and moody. Do you
   A. Realize this is age appropriate and talk to him about it
   B. Ignore it
   C. Promptly decide your child is neurotic and send him to a child psychiatrist
2. Your seven-year-old demands too much of himself, he goes on too long with projects and becomes exhausted. Do you
   A. Talk to him and help him to define stopping points
   B. Ignore it as a trait that will lead to greater accomplishment
   C. Chastise him for stopping even when exhausted
3. He has his good and bad days, some days of high learning and others of forgetting everything. Do you
   A. Shift his intellectual demands on those difficult days
   B. Demand a sugar-free diet and vitamin buildup to ward off bad days
   C. Chastise him
4. Your seven-year-old says he's been picked on by you and, in fact, also by the world at large. Do you
   A. Talk to him about it, giving assurance of your love
   B. Ignore the complaints
   C. Send him to a child psychiatrist because you consider him paranoid
5. Your eight-year-old says, "I can never get anything right, I can't do it." Do you
   A. Sympathize and explain why he does get everything "right" most of the time
   B. Tell him he is talking in a silly fashion
   C. Ignore him
6. Your eight-year-old wants a good relationship with her mother. She sees Mommy kissing Daddy, and feels real jealousy for the attention. Do you

- A. Explain that you love your spouse in a different way from your child but you love them both
- B. Tell her that Daddy is special to you in some way and that she is special to you in other ways and reaffirm your love for her
- C. Ignore her

7. Your eight-year-old had a good beginning on her art project, but then tired and the ending is a disaster. She hates the drawing and in disgust tears it up. Now the child is upset at this self-destruction. Do you
    - A. Plan with her to work on the art in the morning, when she will be able to carry through better, and explain how a success means an awareness of what not to do and this unsatisfactory picture has been its own success
    - B. Sympathize with her, cuddle her, but don't encourage her to redo the drawing for the art project
    - C. Just ignore her as going through another tantrum

The nine-year-old child combines the traits of the two previous years. Your child will have friends and an understanding of the outside world coupled with a quiet introspection. The child is enjoying life but seeks periodic time out to understand what has been experienced.

The nine-year-old has a tendency to become closer to adults. Your child of this age will have a curiosity about your views, the views of your friends, and other adults with whom he or she comes into contact. The physical and emotional development of a nine-year-old also means that there can be genuinely shared interests.

Most nine-year-olds worry greatly about life and their developing skills in whatever areas happen to interest them. When I talk with pediatricians, they all jokingly refer to their nine-year-old patients as neurotics. At times children of this age rebel, often developing very real physical ailments such as an upset stomach when they don't want to do things.

A TEST FOR THE PARENTS OF NINE- TO TEN-YEAR-OLDS

(Score 10 points for A, 5 points for B, and 0 for C)

1. Take a look at the type of artwork your ten-year-old is doing. Most ten-year-olds are taking a serious look at their environments. Younger children draw just from memory and imagination. A ten-year-old has reached the stage where he or she is drawing from life and from memory and imagination.
    A. Are the drawings three-dimensional, showing an attempt to create depth and solidity on the paper? Is there an awareness of perspective? Landscapes might have shading and reveal an understanding of light
    B. Your ten-year-old is still drawing in two dimensions. There is no attempt at shading and creating the illusion of depth. Everything remains a line drawing in outline style
    C. Your child doesn't draw at all
2. When your child listens to music, is he or she
    A. Content with the sound, appreciating whatever style happens to be on. This does not mean he or she has to enjoy what you like. Rather there may be an appreciation for rock but not jazz, classical but not easy listening. Whatever the case, when the child has such music, the music is thoroughly enjoyed
    B. The situation described in answer A is only occasionally true.
    C. It is never true
3. When you tell your ten-year-old to do something, is what you say
    A. "Law." The fact that Mommy or Daddy said to do something is all the motivation needed to go ahead and do it
    B. A cause for rebellion. Your child is perverse. He may do the opposite of what you ask as a gesture of defiance
    C. Your child ignores what you say

4. When it comes to personal happiness, is your ten-year-old
   A. Pleased with life, finding it easy to gain pleasure from his or her general existence most of the time
   B. Occasionally pleased with the world around him
   C. Never very happy
5. When it comes to interpersonal relations, is your ten-year-old
   A. Friendly and nice to others most of the time
   B. Friendly only when it seems to suit his or her needs
   C. Usually not very friendly
6. Academically, does your ten-year-old
   A. Enjoy reading
   B. Reads but only to pass in school
   C. Reads with difficulty, often having trouble concentrating when looking at the printed page
7. In terms of the pursuit of intellectual creativity, does your child
   A. Have a creative imagination which is shown in schoolwork, get good grades, and pursue creative leisure activities rather than passive entertainment such as television
   B. Watch television but is selective about the programs
   C. Use television as a passive outlet for his or her attention, not really caring what is on
8. Around the house, does your ten-year-old
   A. Enjoy helping out when possible
   B. Occasionally help out but most of the time try to "disappear" when he or she suspects that Mommy or Daddy will need help
   C. Never help out and resent the fact that you ask

The average ten-year-old is actually quiet and obedient, and has a sense of self-worth and personal respect. The child's parents are the most important people in his or her eyes and relating to them in a positive way brings pleasure.

The ten-year-old is generally friendly toward others and assumes that they, in turn, will be friendly as well. He is rather matter of fact about life in general, flexible in his activities, and doesn't take anything too seriously. This is usually the period just before changes in growth patterns, hormones, and other factors lead to the problems of adolescence. It is probably the happiest year of childhood for most children because they seem to have the fewest problems with which to cope.

Now that you have a general understanding of the patterns of childhood, patterns which differ from child to child as the years pass, but are general stages of growth, it is time to begin the important goal of making your child exceptional.

Should you confuse behavioral differences with the onset of an illness, the following table will give you an idea of what illnesses are typical at certain ages

Age	Illness
18 months	convulsions may accompany illness with high temperature
21 months	elimination difficulties
two-and-a-half	frequent colds with ear problems, especially with slow-speech children
three	fatigue common
four	colds during winter, coming and going quickly; stomachaches; need to urinate in difficult situations and at mealtimes
five	whooping cough; measles; chicken pox
six	sore throats; allergies; diphtheria; scarlet fever; german measles; mumps
seven	headaches with fatigue; muscular pains; "growing" pains
eight	stomachaches
nine	hands hurt when writing; eyes hurt when reading
ten	no noted illnesses

Note: All these childhood illnesses can be less afflicting with good nutrition and a vitamin supplement.

You may wonder if your children's fears are phobias or just age appropriate and will pass. This table shows some of the common fears which can be expected at various ages.

Age	Fears
two	trains; trucks; thunder; lightning; vacuum cleaner noises; fire crackers; hats; dark colors; toys being moved from usual places or going down the toilet
two-and-a-half	having objects moved to different places; trucks approaching; large objects
three	the "bogeyman"; the dark; animals; mother or father going out at night
four	fire engines; the dark; wild animals; mother leaving, especially at night
five	being bitten by dogs; mother not returning home
six	telephone; ugly voice tones; ghosts; witches; supernatural; someone is "hiding under" bed, etc.
seven	shadows being ghosts; burglars; war; spies; not being liked; being late to school
eight	failure at school; not being loved (fears now become reasonable, mature, and adult)
nine	fear of personal inabilities; fear of school failure
ten	some fear of wild animals; the dark; burglars

There are various phases of intellectual development typical for each age.

Age	Developmental Phases of Intellectual Abilities
12 weeks	social smile; laughs aloud; anticipates eating on sight of food; can sit propped for ten to fifteen minutes
28 weeks	able to sit for short periods of time; can lean forward on hands; grasps objects placed before him; makes vowel sounds

40 weeks	creeps on hands and knees; pokes at small objects with extended forefinger
12 months	vocalizes "Mama" and "Dada" and other words; can walk with one hand to stabilize self; cooperates when dressed
15 months	walks a few steps close to where he can hold on; helps turn pages of a book with supervision; has six words
18 months	walks well; has ten words including names; looks at pictures in books; feeds self
24 months	turns pages of a book; speaks in three-word sentences; has dry pants at night; verbalizes toilet needs; refers to self by name
36 months	can ride tricycle; uses plurals in speech; feeds self; can put on shoes
48 months	can count three objects and point correctly; can wash and dry face and hands; brush teeth; can draw person with two parts (head and legs)
60 months	can count ten objects; can tell how many fingers on each hand; can name penny, nickel, dime, dollar; can name colors correctly; can point out a few letters

A child's intellectual abilities are colored by both his sibling relationships and his ability to obey his parents. Younger children imitate the intellectual drives of their older siblings. If they can obey their parents in executing a command, they have accomplished a degree of mental discipline which is the requirement for developing intellectual abilities.

Here are two tables. One shows the sibling relationship as it varies at different ages. The other shows the ability to obey parents as it varies at different ages.

Age	Changes in Sibling Relationship
two	child gets on better with siblings but is not much interested in them; takes them for granted

Age	
three	relations are better, but teasing and retaliation are the order of the day
four	he is selfish and rough with younger siblings and is overtly jealous of older siblings
five	becomes kind and protective toward younger siblings; starts to play well with older siblings
six	children now tell tales of their siblings; they quarrel with other siblings
seven	plays big brother role to younger siblings; with older siblings there is still jealousy
eight	teasing, quarrelsome with siblings about possessions and privileges
nine	thoughtful and protective, proud of older siblings
ten	more kind and considerate

Note: Now look at your son and realize that what you thought bizarre is really age-appropriate behavior!

Age	Changes in Attitude Toward Obeying Parents
two	child may obey some simple commands but in general is domineering; indirect approaches work better than direct commands
three	more response to directions; likes to please and conform
four	eager to please and conform; likes to do things his own way; enjoys defying adults
five	peaceful; readily obeys
six	responds slowly to commands; he needs time and leeway
seven	does not respond promptly; may forget what you said
eight	finds excuses not to carry out your command but eventually does
nine	responds quickly to obeying your command; sometimes likes to be given detailed instruc-

Age	Changes in Attitude Toward Obeying Parents
	tions to begin with and even then reminded, because his attention, interest, and willingness have not been captured
ten	tens are reasonable and very good about carrying out your commands

Note: This is an age-appropriate average scale.

The information for the lists in this chapter is taken from *Gesell Book of Child Behavior* by Frances Ilg and Louise Ames Bates.

3

Nutrition Makes the Mind Go Round

Nutrition is important to a child's development from birth. This book is not going to tell you that you must switch to some sort of exotic diet. Neither will it tell you that going to a fast-food restaurant on occasion is going to cause your child to become feeble minded. Rather, this chapter will show you what your child needs, how it is obtained, and the reasons why a simple alteration in your child's diet will prepare your child for the achievement of exceptional qualities.

The human body can run, jump, grow, and function even when improperly nourished. However, it cannot function at full capacity without the complete range of nutrients meant to serve as fuel.

Your child must be prepared for learning if he or she is to reach optimum performance. This means having the right kind of nutrients, a diet which permits an increased attention span, improves the ability to think clearly, and insures maximum retention of information.

A tragedy of modern American life is that most of our children have been shortchanged in the growth of mental ability because of the foods they are encouraged to eat. Advertisers and the food industry misrepresent their products and the nutritional worth of their ingredients. Does it really matter that a dozen vitamins and minerals have been added to a loaf of bread if, in the processing of the wheat, sugar, and other ingredients, fifty or more essential nutrients have been removed? Yes, your child is still being shortchanged.

Even the birth of a baby and its early needs are met with false information. A nursing mother is not always encouraged in our society. Nursing is often thought to be a nuisance, especially since many young mothers work. But are the formulas using cow's milk really a proper substitute? A calf weighs ninety pounds at birth and has to be able to stand almost immediately. Give that calf six months and it will weigh 400 pounds. That is a phenomenal growth rate, and a cow's milk is meant to supply the nutrition to meet this need.

The protein found naturally in human mothers' milk is primarily in a form that is extremely easy for the infant to absorb. The kind of protein in a cow's milk is much harder for a human to digest.

The ingredients of a mother's milk vary with the days after birth. When a baby is first born, and for four or five days afterward, the pre-milk, called colostrum, is in the mother's breasts. It provides antibodies to the infant and is high in zinc and choline, essential elements for the child's brain. The fact that it must come from breast feeding is important in another way. Breast feeding results in an emotional bonding between mother and child of invaluable psychological benefits. Breast-fed babies also have fewer allergies and less chance of developing gastroenteritis, a stomach and intestine problem.

Breast-fed babies develop better jaw bone structures because they must suck harder on the breast than on the bottle. They also develop stronger teeth because of the increased calcium. Because of these benefits, not only is it preferable to breast feed your baby if possible, but the breast feeding should continue as long as is practical.

Perhaps the greatest deterrent to exceptional child development is consumption of refined sugar. When something is eaten which lacks all the ingredients necessary for metabolism, it is not a food. It might even be called a "poison" because for it to be digested it must rob one or more organs of their nutrients.

What does this mean for your growing child? Sugar robs the B-complex vitamins from your child's body. The B-complex vitamins serve a broad range of functions which affect your child's nerve tissue, skin, hair, eyes, liver, and other parts of the body. Vitamin B-1, for example, helps combat fatigue, calm your child, and maintain his or her emotions.

Vitamin B-3 is also a calmative. A three-gram dose, when given to an adult, has been found to do exactly the same as ten mg. of the tranquilizer Valium for adults. Your child will need far less than three grams of vitamin B-3, but the end result will be similar.

Vitamin B-6 is called the antiallergy vitamin. Children who have hay fever, asthma, and other stress-aggravated allergies are either not bothered by the problems or have them reduced when they have the right amount of B-6.

A healthy nervous system is assured with vitamin B-12. This vitamin helps build the blood and strengthens the ability to think and function.

Pantothenic acid, still part of B-complex, is also used for fighting stress.

The list of B-complex vitamins goes on, but you can see the point. A child who is lacking in this one essential grouping will have trouble thinking, maintaining adequate stamina to get through the day, learning to coordinate eye-hand movement, and generally will progress a little more slowly. In some cases, children become diagnosed as hyperactive because they are constantly on the move and cannot sit still long enough to be taught. Yet when these children have sugar eliminated from their diet and are given B-complex supplements, they thrive and develop to their capacity, to remain quiet, and learn.

What is so frightening about current societal attitudes, is that the average American child has a diet deficiency. Breakfast is a bowl of sugar-coated corn flakes which have been processed to the point where a corn kernel's normal nutritional value is almost completely destroyed. Sweet rolls and doughnuts are common staples because they taste good and are filling. Unfortunately they are also loaded with sugar, fat, and other ingredients of little or no nutritional value. With white bread the wheat's true value is destroyed by refinement and removal.

How many children grab hamburgers with a cheese substitute loaded with chemicals, perhaps artificial color, and processed condiments? There is sugar in the pickles, the bun has both sugar and refined flour, and the french fries and soft drink both add sugar and greatly limit nutrition. A whole baked potato, including the skin, is a rich source of vitamins. But the bulk of the vitamins are in the skin. Cut that away, slice the potato, drown it in a deep-fat fryer, and you are left with something which fills children's stomachs but reduces their ability to learn.

Often the food we feed our children is processed, frozen, canned, preserved, and laced with chemical additives and food dyes. If candy, cake, pie, or other sweets are rewards for "cleaning your plate," even a truly nutritious meal is defeated because the high quantity of sugar will "steal" the nutrients the body would gain.

You, the parent, must keep in mind that if your child enjoys good nutrition now, the advice here will make improvements. If your child's diet needs to be changed, following the nutritional guidelines in this chapter will end many learning problems, making it possible to move toward the exceptional range.

The first step in every household is to remove the maximum amount of sugar and white flour from the family diet. Ideally this means complete elimination of these items. For example, when you prepare a hamburger, you have a good meal if you use real cheese, not processed spread, good quality ground beef, and a whole wheat bun. Most large supermarkets sell whole wheat hamburger buns, without sugar or chemical preservatives. These can be stored in a refrigerator or freezer to keep them from becoming dry. Catsup should be eliminated because of its high—as much as fifty percent—sugar content.

What happens when sugar and white flour remain in the diet? Researchers have found that most children complain of anxiety, depression, insomnia, inability to concentrate, restlessness, difficulty in learning—a total of thirty complaints can be listed. This is why I put so much emphasis on nutrition here.

Certain rules should be followed when planning your child's diet. Do not use sweets as a reward. Buy or make plain, natural yogurt, then sweeten it with honey and pureed fruits. It is far less expensive than commercial fruit yogurt, much of which is sweetened with sugar. (There are different types of sugar and the one the brain needs—glucose—is manufactured by the body. This naturally created body sugar is converted from your food's nutrients. It has nothing to do with the intake of the various added sugars.)

Breakfasts can work around the commercials. Raw oatmeal is delicious eaten cold with milk. Or try granola moistened with unsweetened apple juice. Unsweetened fruit juice should be substituted for soft drinks, fruit punch, and "fruit" drinks. Read the labels. If there is sucrose, sugar, corn syrup, or corn sweeteners, the most common ways of saying the same thing—this beverage is loaded with sugar—then you do not want it. The added sweeteners mean you are limiting your child's potential by leaching out vital vitamins and minerals. Usually the loss is with the B-complex vitamins, manganese, and zinc, so vital for the many processes involved in proper brain functioning.

Among other popular foods which can contribute to poor diet are potato chips, corn chips, cheese chips, and similar items fried in hydrogenated fats. Hydrogenation is a convenient process used by the food industry to package oils so they become solid fats. This is the method of manufacture which makes peanut butter and salad dressings look smooth and consistent in texture. It also destroys the essential fatty acids necessary for healthy heart and body circulation. Look on the label to be certain these fats are not present.

Most hot dogs and most packaged cold cuts have so many preservatives and dyes among the additives that they are going to slow your child's development. It has been found that a child's absorption of dyes will inhibit the learning process.

Even a child with a high level of proper nutrition can still benefit from vitamin, mineral, and food supplements. Every child should have a good multivitamin-mineral tablet each morning after eating. Avoid vitamins with sugar.

There are two types of vitamins, those that are fat soluble and therefore stored in body fat, and those that are water soluble, excreted daily in all our wastes. The water soluble are more fragile and must be replaced daily. Such water-soluble vitamins include all the B-complex vitamins and vitamin C. There is no danger of overdosing with water-soluble vitamins because any excess is expelled daily with urine and perspiration. By contrast, the few fat-soluble vitamins—A and D—can have a toxic effect when taken in excess. They stay in the body, accumulating if you take more than you really need.

The proper way to deal with the question of vitamin dosage is to restrict your child's vitamin A and vitamin D supplement to the daily multivitamin tablet. The amount of these vitamins obtained naturally through both food and sunshine will not cause any problems. However, you can safely vary the dosage of the B-complex and C vitamins according to the specific body requirements of your child.

Your child needs the natural vitamin D obtained from sunlight. The light receptors in the back of the eye convert natural light, through a process called photobiology, which is a natural tranquilizer. This is why both children and adults should be exposed to at least a half hour of exercise in the sunlight each day. This will help your child to be more relaxed, alert, and able to learn.

These same photoreceptors in the back of the eye stimulate the entire endocrine system, and a hormone that, it is suspected, influences mood and many other body functions. The vitamin D produced from the skin's exposure to the sun is essential to the absorbtion and metabolism of calcium. Jane Brody has reported in the *New York Times* that there have been preliminary studies suggesting problems of fatigue, decreased performance, diminished immunological defenses, reduced physical fitness, depression, and sleeping trouble are a result of overexposure to incandescent and fluorescent lighting that lack the full spectrum of natural light. Dr. John Ott's studies show that children exposed to excessive amounts of television while seated too close to the screen, have behavioral problems and impaired learning ability.

Children must be exposed to natural sunlight if you want them to perform at their best behavior and learning levels.

What are other natural sources of vitamins A and D? Carrots, sweet potatoes, spinach, beets, lettuce, liver, eggs, peaches, apricots, squash, and dairy products.

Vitamin D can be obtained in fish oil, available in capsule form.

In addition to the vitamin supplements, the essential B vitamins are found in wheat germ, whole wheat bread, nuts, meat, fish, cheese, eggs, fowl, brewer's yeast, green leafy vegetables, animal protein, and other sources. You can see that even children who are fussy eaters are going to find foods that they like which supply this nutrition.

Pantothenic acid is a B-complex vitamin sold separately. It is related to the chemical cortisone and can both prevent and treat arthritis in children. It is naturally found in legumes, eggs, pork, mushrooms, broccoli, cauliflower, beef, and other foods.

Folic acid is important, yet such small quantities are needed to insure proper blood development and growth that often the combination of a proper diet and a vitamin supplement provides necessary amounts. Certified raw cow's milk, some pasteurized milk, green leafy vegetables, whole grains, tuna fish, dates, and organ meats such as liver, are among the sources.

Biotin, part of the B-complex vitamin, is excellent for the lungs of a child with allergies, asthma, and other problems. It can reduce dry skin, eczema, and similar difficulties. It is easily obtained in the foods already recommended, but should be increased when your child is sick and given antibiotics. Biotin is normally manufactured inside the body by essential bacteria found in the intestinal tract. Antibiotics given for various illnesses that are normal to childhood growth also kill both good bacteria, which manufactures biotin as part of its work, and the bad bacteria which cause illness. The biotin needs replacement at such times and a biotin vitamin supplement will replenish the need.

Inositol, a natural calmative, excellent for sleeping problems, is another of the B-complex vitamins which is obtained from normal diets. It is most common in citrus fruits, brewer's yeast, meat, nuts, and milk.

You have probably used a vitamin called PABA (para-amino benzoic acid) with great frequency if you go swimming, hiking, or engage in other outdoor activities. This is because it is the sun screen found in protective lotions and tanning compounds. When taken internally, it also protects against harmful sun radiation. It also has the side effect of reducing your child's fatigue, and overcoming depression and irritability when combined with the other B-complex vitamins. It is most commonly found in wheat germ, organ meats, and brewer's yeast.

Choline is one of the most exciting of the B-complex vitamins because it can affect your child's health, speed of learning, ability to apply both physical and mental skills, and influence other areas of his or her life. It also counters the bad effects of some pharmaceuticals. It revitalizes the nerve synapses which send various messages from the brain to the body, making your normal child respond with exceptional speed. It aids memory and has been used successfully in my practice with adults when they are giving up tranquilizers, cigarettes, alcohol, and drugs. Choline eliminates the cravings which occur during withdrawal and helps restore the mind to peak efficiency.

Your baby is especially susceptible to choline deficiency. Frequently I have seen mothers who think they are feeding their babies properly but are unknowingly depriving the infants of choline. The baby seems normal, though somewhat thin, irritable, and less able to do things than others his or her age. When choline is added, through the addition of brewer's yeast, lecithin, wheat germ, egg yolks, or organ meats such as liver, the baby changes to a happy, stronger, healthier looking child in just a day or two.

Lecithin is excellent for memory and is a natural nerve tonic and calmative. Lecithin granules are also delicious. All the children for whom I have suggested them love their nutty flavor. One teaspoonful makes 500 mg. of choline. You can sprinkle it on breakfast foods, mix it with fruit, or add it to milk, shaking the liquid to create a drink they will see as a treat.

Vitamin C is essential to your child's health and learning abilities. Your child will have allergies reduced, fewer colds, infrequent nosebleeds, stronger cell walls, and increased stamina. Cholesterol buildup is eliminated by vitamin C, preventing hardening of the arteries. A child with inadequate vitamin C will show heart, artery, and blood changes associated with someone in their forties.

Emotional and physical stress is a major factor in the loss of vitamin C. Remember that stress varies with the individual. The first day at school, a trip to a relative, planning to attend a party, facing a trip to the doctor or dentist, illness, and other factors are all stressful for your child. Whatever quantity of vitamin C he or she normally needs to get through the day disappears almost instantly at such time. Your child's body will need five to ten times the normal amount of vitamin C to handle very stressful experiences.

Oranges, grapefruit, parsley, mustard greens, green peppers, and other foods all contain vitamin C. Be certain to read the labels of fruit juices, though. Some are sweetened with sugar.

Vitamin E may be one of the most important vitamins you can give your child, especially if you live in urban or smog-covered areas. This vitamin, once in the bloodstream, attacks pollutants, chemical waste in food, liquids, and the air when they enter your child's body. Vitamin E lessens the chance of clogged blood vessels. You can break vitamin E capsules and rub them into burns to promote healing. This vitamin, along with the mineral magnesium, is beneficial for cramps. Without vitamin E, vitamin A would not be fully absorbed in the body. However, vitamin E should be taken a few hours before or after any iron is taken since taking them close together reduces both their effectiveness.

Vitamin E is found naturally in whole grains, legumes, and nuts. The requirements for vitamin E vary with geography. If the air is polluted, there is chemical waste in your water, and foods grown in the ground are exposed to harmful levels of pesticides and fertilizers, the need for vitamin E should be greater than in a rural area where you eat vegetables grown in your own organic garden.

Vitamin K is manufactured from healthful bacteria found in the intestines. It is so easily created through the metabolism of food that supplements are almost never needed. This vitamin is especially helpful with the coagulation of blood.

Fatty acids are usually avoided in diets, since what few fatty acids are necessary are manufactured by the human body. When your child does seem to need these, such as when dry skin, brittle hair and nails, or similar problems appear, foods such as wheat germ, safflower, soy, and corn oils, and sunflower seeds all provide the necessary amount. Two-percent milk—a homogenized milk and skim milk—also works well.

There are six nutrients that our bodies need: protein, carbohydrates, oil, vitamins, minerals, and water. The least acknowledged is minerals.

Minerals regulate the flow of bodily fluids. They have the power to maintain the delicate internal water balance needed for all mental and physical processes. Through osmosis, the minerals draw substances into and out of our cells. Minerals have the power to rejuvenate us, strengthen us, grow new hair, regulate our heartbeat, improve our thinking power, and build a dynamic memory by liberating the vitamins in our body to do their work. If minerals are not present, other elements cannot be assimilated.

Calcium has many important functions in the body. One of the most important is helping to transport nerve impulses from one part of the body to another. Calcium builds and maintains strong bones and teeth. Food sources of calcium include: milk, cheese, egg yolk, molasses, almonds, sesame seeds, brussels sprouts, sardines, oysters, collards, and turnip greens. In order for calcium to be utilized effectively, vitamins A, C, D, and phosphorous must be present.

The easiest way to correct a calcium deficiency is through the supplement dolomite (natural calcium and magnesium). Read the label, though. What you want is calcium and magnesium that is found naturally. Some products labeled dolomite actually contain other ingredients including flavoring and colorings to which some children are allergic. Bone meal and calcium tablets also handle any deficiency.

The use of dolomite as a supplement has an added benefit. It helps you relax and your child will sleep better at night with this supplement. In Chapter 8 I will discuss the effect dolomite has for insomnia.

The magnesium in dolomite (two parts calcium to one part magnesium) serves an essential purpose for your child. In combination with vitamin B-6, it can improve your child's memory and also his or her comprehension. It calms your child when restless and is also effective with hyperactivity, should that ever be a problem for you. Magnesium also affects a small child's ability to get through the night without wetting the bed.

Magnesium is important for both growth and the general way the body handles stress. Food sources are lima beans, oatmeal, almonds, whole wheat flour, brown rice, leafy vegetables, grapefruit, unrefined vegetable oils, dark green vegetables, molasses, and seafood among others. Magnesium is destroyed by food processing.

Zinc is a surprisingly important nutrient for the exceptional child. It affects growth, the ability of the body to heal, and that scourge of adolescence—acne—is usually nothing more than a zinc deficiency. Among the food sources are organ meats, wheat bran, wheat germ, milk, brewer's yeast, eggs, onions, nuts, and leafy greens.

Minerals and vitamins must be linked together in the body for each to be assimilated. For example, vitamin A is needed to help zinc function properly. Zinc is also needed with vitamin B to handle metabolism.

Iron is needed for the manufacture of red blood cells. When your child drinks large quantities of cow's milk, iron is often lacking. Thus food is a good source, with a reliance upon raisins, eggs, wheat germ, liver, seeds, almonds, barley, bananas, brewer's yeast, meats, leafy vegetables, prunes, and other foods. Dessicated liver is a good supplemental source.

Manganese is a mineral of vital importance to the diet. It helps to nourish the nerves and brain. It aids in the transmittal of messages among the brain, nerves, and muscles throughout the body. A shortage is frequently responsible for what are diagnosed as epileptic seizures in children. Fortunately many of the foods already mentioned are rich in manganese. These include nuts, wheat germ, legumes, seeds, oatmeal, corn, beets, and onions, among others.

Sodium, as found in table salt, is needed but overused by most parents. Your child's ability to maintain a sound cardiovascular system is dependent upon limiting salt intake. Usually a craving for salt represents a zinc deficiency, not a need for more sodium in the diet. Foods such as meat have a natural abundance of sodium. Salt cravings frequently reflect stress which disappears with stress-handling vitamins added to the diet. These include the C and B-complex vitamins along with the zinc. Natural sources of sodium include kelp, celery, romaine, watermelon, and seafood.

Potassium, chromium, iodine, copper, chlorine, sulphur, silicon, molybdenum, cobalt, and selenium are trace minerals needed by your children. Most of these are obtained by eating the foods mentioned. The one exception is iodine which occasionally has to be added in the form of an extremely moderate amount of iodized salt for people living far from sea water.

Copper plumbing in older buildings releases more copper into the water than may be beneficial to your system. This can lead to copper poisoning which is manifested in depression. This is why I recommend a water purifier to anyone who suspects they or their children may be having this problem.

Because minerals can affect the biochemical balances, it is important to give your child a multimineral tablet with modest proportions of each mineral rather than attempting to self-prescribe.

In the Appendix of this book is a guide to the general nutritional needs for your exceptional child. It covers the basic growing years and beyond. By following the recommendations, modifying the vitamins according to your child's unique body needs and lifestyle, you will be able to help your child reach full mental and physical potential.

Remember that an exceptional child starts with proper nutrition—the tool to enabling his or her body to function at peak efficiency. Whether your child is an infant or approaching the teenage years, the altering of his or her diet to ensure maximum mental efficiency is the best way to start your program to make your child exceptional. A well-balanced diet and a daily vitamin and mineral supplement are what I recommend.

4

Mind Games Are as Much Fun as Toy Games

There are both mental and physical ways to expand your child's imagination. This chapter explores those tools that are important in your child's mental development.

There are two aspects of raising children. One is loving discipline, restricting the physical boundaries of existence for your child's protection. Your toddler may be fascinated by a small animal darting about in a vacant field across the street. Watching the animal up close might be excellent for his or her growth, but if getting there means running across the street through traffic, you will of course refuse to let the toddler yield to that desire.

You want your child to be curious, but you don't want that curiosity to become self-destructive. Setting limits for the child's own protection is essential. They both keep your child alive and begin to strengthen your child's understanding of survival.

The second aspect of child rearing frees your child from all limits. It is meant to send your child's mind soaring beyond all restrictions. It will explode his or her creative potential, helping to develop exceptional qualities beyond your greatest expectations. It requires providing a free but safe physical environment from the time a child is very small and an unlimited mental stimulation for total creative expansion.

The exceptional child is one who is encouraged to explore his or her environment without restrictions. If your child is just learning to crawl, child-proof a room so that there is nothing harmful within. Then let your baby roam free, crawling under and over tables, exploring different objects, fingering, touching, tasting, and generally getting into everything. That which can be damaged or harmful has been removed, so there is no reason to say "no" to anything. Your baby is encouraged to learn the full extent of his or her environment, finding excitement in everything new and different.

The adventures of a baby roaming at will within a living room, family room, or other area do not seem very important to most parents. It seems to be little more than meaningless mischief. However, this random play is what will make your baby want to learn, to explore, and to understand the environment. The curiosity which develops carries over into the older child, resulting in an inquiring mind.

Certainly there is a time when you must say "no." But to nurture the exceptional qualities, you should try to keep your infant where he or she will not have to be stopped, where each new discovery can be the start of an exciting adventure rather than a scolding.

Suppose there are two infants, Mary and Suzie, both with exceptional potential. From the onset of Mary's mobility, she is allowed the run of the baby-proofed room. She sees a long ear sticking up from the couch, touches it, pulls on it, and eventually dislodges a stuffed toy rabbit that was almost completely hidden by the cushions. She is delighted and begins to gain an understanding of how to anticipate a whole object from the sighting of a single part. She is constantly learning, seeking new items and experiences, then growing in sophistication as she gains an understanding that there can be more to a subject, object, or issue than just what is obvious on the surface.

Suzie is raised differently. No child-proofing is done when she is a toddler so she constantly is told "no." She is not allowed to touch the coffee cup on the table because the hot liquid will burn her. She is not allowed in a cabinet because the cleaning supplies will hurt her. She cannot use her mouth on the edge of the chest of drawers because it is an antique. There are toys to enjoy and acceptable areas for her to roam in, but she hears the word "no" far more than encouragement to explore unrestricted. The world to her seems perilous and untouchable.

Suzie and Mary grow up. Both do very well in school. Both go to college and then on to graduate school in medicine. Both become doctors, yet there the similarities end. Suzie is an excellent technician. She applies what she has learned and keeps up with the latest research through medical journals. She is bright, competent, and respected.

Mary is also successful, yet Mary's mind has been trained with the exceptional quality of intellectual curiosity. She does not just apply what she has learned, she questions whether or not there is a better way to handle patients, a more certain method for combating illness. Mary enters medical research, discovering answers to questions once unanswerable and seeking better ways to help the sick. She applies her creativity to the field and lets this exceptional quality take her to higher levels of medicine.

The early restrictions, the constant repetition of "no," has made Suzie an obedient adult whose mind has narrowed its focus. She carries over into adulthood a desire not to offend. She will not try something until it has been approved by others. She is an excellent professional but she lacks the intellectual spark of Mary.

The smaller your child is, the longer it will seem to take for exceptional qualities to emerge from your actions. However, the effect is real and long lasting. Talking in an adult manner to an infant results in sophisticated, exceptional verbal skills when the child does begin to talk. Letting your crawling child roam free, within safe confines, eventually translates into a probing mind that is not afraid to explore the unknown.

There are times when a child must be reprimanded. Small children frequently test the boundaries of what is safe. You cannot stand by and watch a toddler try to stick a hairpin into an electric outlet. At the same time, you must adopt the attitude that every positive accomplishment is a good one, even when the action could have been better.

For example, take the case of Billy, who was eight and a half when he came to see me. Billy was an adorable little boy with tousled black hair, a shirt which kept coming out of his pants, and alert eyes which seemed to study and analyze everything in my office. He was bright and extremely alert, yet he was not going forward in school. The way he kept his shoulders hunched forward and his eyes averted from me when he became aware that I was watching seemed to indicate a certain dislike of himself.

Billy was one of six children and I began asking him about the enjoyable times he had with his family. Usually he mentioned times when he was close to his parents, when they gave him special attention, such as helping him learn to swim when they went to the California coast. I noticed that he always seemed to talk of periods when both his parents paid attention to him. He was not jealous of his many brothers and sisters, so much as desirous of having his own time and space with them.

Finally I asked Billy what he did to create love. "What do you do to get that special time you want, that time with your Mommy and Daddy? What do you create?"

"Failure," he said, speaking barely in a whisper. "When I do badly in school, Mommy and Daddy give me more attention." Billy was shocked by what he had said. He looked at me with eyes wide with surprise. He had verbalized feelings he never faced before.

"I like school," said Billy. "I really learn all sorts of neat things. But when I take a test, I always forget everything until after it's over. Then I know what mistakes I made but it's too late. When I get my bad grade, my Mommy and Daddy yell at me and talk with me about doing better. I guess I don't like doing bad on the tests but Mommy and Daddy wouldn't care about me if I got good grades."

I had Billy tell his parents what he had just told me. I also talked with them about their problems. Both of them had responsible careers and they had five other children to handle. What they did not realize was that they had used negative discipline to raise them and this was preventing Billy from reaching his full potential. They felt they had to show displeasure when one of their children did poorly and they would take time to explain why they were angry, why they felt the children should be doing better.

I told Billy's parents to stop giving negative reinforcement to Billy and the other children. I had them ignore his failings and praise that which he did well. If he had a ten-question quiz and he missed eight questions, they were to praise him for the wonderful way he answered the two that were right. The failings were not mentioned.

Billy's parents also had a family discussion with all the children. They explained how much they were all loved and how they, the parents, did not have much free time at home. They said that they would divide their time so the other children had their own times to talk, read, share, walk, or do anything else with each parent each day. The family would also take time together for the same thing. Then, whenever one of the children needed more attention, that child only had to ask.

"The change in Billy and the others is remarkable, Dr. Green," said Janet a month later. "We did what you suggested. We stopped mentioning Billy's bad grades or his mistakes. We ignored them and praised what he did well. At first we felt a little foolish. He was failing so badly that some papers left little to praise. One time we had to just tell him how much his penmanship had improved.

"We also told Billy that he should ask when he needed extra time with us, and he began doing that a few times. He never intruded on time for the others but might come to us after he should have been in bed or during some similar period. He would say he was feeling lonely or scared and we would talk and hold him. When he realized he was special in a positive way, he stopped acting the way he had. He's now getting perfect papers and the other children's grades have improved. The teachers say it's a remarkable change, that they're finding our children truly exceptional and they can't understand why. They don't realize that the answer is positive reinforcement."

The use of fantasy is a critical factor for creating an exceptional child. For example, when your child develops an imaginary friend, and almost all children do, encourage that friend. Ask about the friend, learn his or her family history, what the friend does, and other details. Include the friend in your family's plans. You are not ensuring that your child will develop abnormally by making the false into something real. Rather you are helping to expand your child's creative horizons by encouraging the full utilization of his or her imagination in a way that is perfectly natural.

Small children of around four or five will occasionally use *illogic* to try and avoid punishment for something they have done wrong. This is different from an imaginary friend and should not be encouraged. For example, suppose you walk into the living room and discover your prize antique vase shattered on the floor. Your little girl is standing terrified, holding a small ball she was warned not to play with in the house. If you react by saying, "Who knocked over this vase?" your daughter is liable to say, "Johnny down the street did it." You know full well that Johnny has been away from your home for two days, your daughter is holding the ball, and the ball shows evidence of having hit something.

The best way to handle this problem is with logic. It is better not to give your child an out when the evidence is clear. You should say, "I am disappointed that you played with your ball inside the house when I told you not to do that. Now you have broken my vase because you disobeyed. You can see why I didn't want you playing with that in here. You have done a bad thing and I want you to promise that you will never make this mistake again. The ball is to be used outside only." However, if you make the mistake of giving your child that escape of blaming someone else, rational logic will stop the attempt to shift the blame.

"I don't see how Johnny could have hit the vase," you might say. "Johnny hasn't been over here today. I was only gone a few minutes but I saw Johnny playing in his yard (or at the store or whatever). Since you are the only one here, and since you are holding the ball, I think that you were the one who hit the vase. Isn't that correct?"

"But, Johnny . . ."

"No, Johnny didn't hit it. You did. You disobeyed me and played with that ball in the house. I told you not to do that because you can break things with it. I am disappointed that you disobeyed me this time and I want you to promise you won't make this mistake again."

Your child should not be punished for trying to put the blame on someone else. It is enough to correct the child's assertion and make it clear that it is important to take responsibility for personal actions. This is very different from having an imaginary friend, even though there may be times when the child wants the imaginary friend to have made the mistake.

Create fantasy games to further the positive imagination within your child. For example, when one of our children turned two, my wife and I often had a hard time calming him before bedtime. This is a common problem because small children will often go until they drop. I decided to create a game which would both strengthen his imagination and lead to the self-creation of a feeling of serenity.

First I pretended to eat an apple. I held up my hand and shaped it as though I was holding something and explained to my son that I had an apple. Then I took a bite from it, began chewing and used my facial expression to show how much I was enjoying it.

"Now you take an apple from this bowl," I said to my son, handing him an imaginary bowl of fruit. He was delighted and took what I'm sure, in his mind, was the largest apple of them all. Then he delighted in taking a giant bite, chewing happily, all the time giggling at the fun and silliness.

Next we each ate an imaginary banana, peeling the skins and having a grand time getting rid of them. We followed this with an imaginary bunch of grapes. Then, with my son thoroughly involved, I said, "Now we are going to have some peace."

My son was puzzled. "Peace, Daddy? A piece of what?"

"Peace," I repeated, beginning to pantomime what I was trying to get him to do. I put my fingers to my lips and softly said, "Sh . . . Sh . . . Hush . . . Hush . . . Peace . . . Quiet . . ." I closed my eyes, smiled, and pretended to be completely at rest. I slowed my breathing, inhaling through my nose, exhaling through my mouth. Then I slowly opened my eyes and repeated the word "peace."

"Can I have some peace, Daddy?"

"Just take some," I said, watching as my two-year-old imitated me.

He forced himself to be quiet, to rest. The real exhaustion he was feeling seemed to overwhelm him. He relaxed, smiling, calming his body and his mind with the fantasy game.

My son and I played this game with some frequency. He loved the pretending and the relaxed feeling he got when eventually we shared some "peace." We reached the point where I would calm him at bedtime by just suggesting that he give himself peace when he was a little restless.

I then took this game to the parents in my practice. I taught it both to them and their children, and they all have found that it is extremely effective. Their children love the special attention the game provides, and taking peace gives them a sense of serenity which is very calming.

Games like this are fine, but I don't have a great deal of time, you may be telling yourself. I want my child to be exceptional. I love my child and want the best, but I owe myself some time. I need to rest when I've had a hard day. I can't spend every free moment playing these games.

This is a natural reaction and quite true. Parents have emotional burdens. They must deal with coworkers, spouses, bills, and numerous other considerations. However, you will find that you do not need to work with your child on fantasy games every day. You also do not need to be actively involved every time your child learns to do them for him- or herself.

Your child only can be exceptional with your involvement. However, as I said earlier, it is not the amount of time you spend but the quality of that time. If you have just twenty minutes a day on the average and your child has your full attention during that period, the value of that short interaction will be great. It is so far beyond what the majority of children receive that it will have the desired effect of bringing forth the exceptional qualities in your child.

Children around three years of age love fairy tales in which men and women show exceptional qualities of heroism and bravery when faced with overwhelming opposition. The stories may be exaggerated fantasies but the qualities depicted are not. The dragon you want your child eventually to face may be the adversities he or she will face in the world of business or medicine or law. You want your child to learn to summon the inner courage of a knight in armor when your child must face a problem that is frightening. You want to develop attitudes and inner strengths that are the real subjects of these stories.

When you read these fairy stories to your children, decide which of the characters is most worth imitation. Then substitute your child's name for that hero when you relate the story to your child. As you read directly from the book, or verbally relate it from memory, the substitution should be made each time the person is named. This will create positive self-images.

Always try to discuss these stories with your child when you are through with the reading. "What would you do when faced with a fierce dragon? How would you save the kingdom from destruction?" Or whatever questions seem appropriate. You can also use this technique to help your child deal with personal fears, whether it is the nursery school bully, the periodic visits to the dentist, or something equally terrifying for your child. Perhaps it has overwhelmed the child in "real" life but the child who has creatively expanded his or her mind through your talking can act in the manner of the hero or heroine. The exceptional qualities are both perceived and applied. The fantasy thus has a broader meaning and takes root in the subconscious. Such children will come to know that handling any crisis is possible because they know they have the resources, and this makes the exceptional child courageous and inventive even though still quite small.

The fantasy game involving the fairy tale hero or heroine also helps bring you and your child closer together. Earlier in this chapter I mentioned the problem of negativism. Here we have an example of positive reinforcement. The parent is saying, in effect, "I respect you. I believe in your abilities. To me, you have the potential for being one of these heroes." It is a warm, loving reaction which subtly bonds you and your child.

Some fantasy games have been made such an integral part of our ordinary childhood that we do not realize their importance. For example, peek-a-boo actually teaches your child that loved ones do not disappear. For a small child, having the eyes closed and the object hidden from view means that it's gone forever. The loss is actually quite frightening. Thus the extreme joy when the eyes are uncovered and there is the loved one.

The same is true with the game of hiding a stuffed toy, so that only a hand, a tail, or some other part is seen. The child not only satisfies his or her curiosity, the child also sees that an object has many parts. You can identify a larger whole by just seeing a portion of the object and you can find that there is more to something than just what is visible, both important lessons in life that are usually learned much later.

For older children, the games must be deliberate. For example, when your child is around six, it is possible to convey very sophisticated ideas that develop selected exceptional qualities. A child of this age understands creativity. A possible game to enhance this is the following.

"What does creativity mean to you?" you might ask the child.

"Isn't that when I draw something or play on the piano? That's creative, isn't it?"

"What sort of drawing are you talking about?" I asked a boy. Your questions should gradually narrow your child's thinking until he or she is expressing ideas clearly.

"When I draw, I feel good about the drawing," he said. He explained how he liked creating what an adult might call a harmonious picture. It was the same with the piano. He played with the sounds until he found tones that seemed to go together. They had a harmony to them even though they did not relate to a song someone had written. He had gone from just banging to finding combinations of notes which sounded enjoyable together. It is the discovery of this harmony in art, in music, and in life which develops the exceptional qualities of creativity. Once this discovery is made, the child can go on to what adults would feel are true creations, full musical arrangements, and the like.

Each time your child tries drawing, playing with sounds, or otherwise being creative, encourage the activity. If you lack a musical instrument in your home and you do not feel your child would seriously study one, create your own. Fill glasses of water to different levels and have your child play music by tapping the sides with a spoon or wetting the rim and running a finger around it. Or take a cardboard tube from a toilet paper or paper towel roll, put a piece of wax paper over one end, securing it with a rubber band, punch holes along one end of the cardboard (start with four and go to a maximum of eight), then give it to your child. Have your child cover three of the holes with his or her fingers. Then have your child blow through the uncovered tube opening, using a buzzing sound. Have your child keep making the sound while covering and uncovering different holes. Each change of holes will change the pitch of the sound.

Musical instrument traditionalists may remember a piece of toilet paper, wrapping it once around the teeth of a comb, then blowing through it. You change the sound by singing through it, the tissue paper-comb combination altering the pitch.

Take a six-pack of empty pop bottles and fill them to varying levels with water, much like the glasses. This time, instead of hitting them, have your child blow across the lips of the bottles. Six different tones can be played, with higher and lower sounds created by altering the water level in the bottles.

Old pots and pans can make musical instruments. Use a wooden spoon for the beater so that different tones can be created. The purpose is not to make noise but to teach your child to work with different sounds, putting them together in play so that they have a harmonious quality. When you show your child that different sounds can be made, he or she will naturally seek to make them harmonious.

In these ways, your child will come to an understanding of what creativity means. The fact that you have been praising the efforts and the genuine improvements in creative achievement, no matter how simple they may seem, has made your child feel good about creativity as a goal. This is an important exceptional trait. With a positive attitude, you can then begin to use fantasy games to strengthen the achievement.

The simplest fantasy game also crosses into the realm of meditation for children, a subject I will discuss in greater detail in the next chapter. Basically meditation for children involves helping them change their brain wave patterns. At different times, everyone has different brain waves, the most important being alpha and theta. These are the brain waves achieved when a mind is at peace, something both adults and children can learn to do through the techniques in this book. At alpha, a positive image is introduced which can give your child exceptional goals as well as the ability to focus his or her full attention on achieving them. Theta waves, achieved with this same exercise, can lead to what often have been called paranormal phenomena. They also can be used to trigger positive behavioral and personality changes and the rapid development of exceptional qualities. For now we will be concerned with just one exercise related to the fantasy games under discussion.

Have your child lie down on the floor, a couch, or wherever else he or she is comfortable. Tell your child to think about his or her body. "Think of your toes. Feel them relaxing. They feel good. They are resting. You are happy with the way they feel.

"Now think of your feet. They are relaxing. They feel good. That good feeling has traveled from your toes, through your feet and is now going to your ankles. Up your legs, past your knees." You keep talking about how relaxed your child feels, how much at peace. Your child's eyes should be closed and you should have your child slow her breathing. Continue having the child think of the different body parts as they relax, working all the way to the top of her head.

Repeat this fractional relaxation exercise at least once a day until your child can do it alone. This will get your child into the alpha state and make him or her feel good. Then you take this exercise a step further to the point where it will have the positive effect you want. This is the fantasy part which leads to exceptional growth.

"Now that you're relaxed, I want you to picture yourself drawing the picture you always wanted to draw," you will say to your child. If your child is musical, then the allusion will be to music. If your child does many things in creative fields, you might want to alternate. It does not matter, so long as your child is guided toward positive imagery in whatever ways are appealing.

"You know how much fun you have being creative," you might say. "I want you to imagine what you look like having fun drawing a picture. Now I want you to make your mind like a television camera.

Zoom in for a close-up of yourself so that you can see the details of the picture you are drawing. It is the best picture you have ever done. It is the most original, the most beautiful. It is a picture people might want to own in their own homes, people who don't even know you, but who see how creative you are being. Can you see yourself making this picture?"

Your child will agree.

"Now I want you to take this picture and pull it inside yourself. Pretend that this picture is actually becoming a part of you. It is as if your body has opened and this image of yourself drawing this beautiful picture is coming inside of you.

"As you bring this picture into you, don't you feel even more creative? Do you feel as though you are getting better and better, more creative than you have ever been before? Maybe your next picture won't be quite that good and maybe it will be better. If the next picture isn't like that, then maybe the one after it or the one after that will be. You have become more creative and you will soon see this as you continue drawing. This will make you even happier than you are now. Don't you feel wonderful?"

Your child agrees. His or her mind is able to fantasize this image very easily. All human beings have the mental ability to create strong visual images. Most adults see these as flights of fancy which have to be discouraged. However, exceptional adults use them for creative ends—the development of new inventions, medicines, cures for disease, business concepts, and other work which advances society. A child who is encouraged toward this end becomes exceptional and carries this into adulthood. Your encouragement is both natural and tremendously beneficial for your child.

Next have your child visualize this creative process all around him. "I want you to see yourself doing this wonderful drawing and hold this image of you drawing a great picture in front of your body. Now let the image move closer until it enters you and is part of you. Then see it behind you the same way and pull it into your body. See it on your right side, your left side, above your head, and below your feet. Each time, pull it in to you so that you feel the wonderful experience filling your whole body.

"It is a happy time for you. You are growing in your creativity. You feel good about yourself. You are relaxed and happy."

Eventually you will want your child to do this on her own. She will be saying to herself, "I am creative. I am happy. I am loved." Or whatever else is appropriate. This same method can even be used to prepare for an important test in school (studying has to be done, too, of course). "I am well prepared. I know the material. I will answer the questions correctly. My teacher will be pleased." Visualizations vastly improve self-confidence and help to make the self-image more positive.

Tom, a child of ten who lacked self-confidence, was withdrawn and consequently daydreamed in school and got poor marks. Using the visualization techniques I've described, I was able to help Tom achieve a positive and aggressively improved performance in school. His internal self-image improved so he could translate it externally. Tom was able to bring his grades from a C level to an A level, to his parents' and teachers' amazement.

School-age children can combine fantasy games with structured learning experiences. For example, suppose you have a child who has difficulty with math but is fascinated by playing with an airplane. You can change that problem area into a strength through a fantasy game. You may need a little help from your child's teacher, but this should not be difficult. Most teachers are delighted with parental involvement in education.

Your child should fantasize being an airplane pilot. He has to "fly" across the room or from one room to the next. You can set up schedules, determine the distance (one foot of floor space can be made to equal a mile or ten miles or even 100 miles), and decide the speed the plane is flying. Then you can do simple math problems or more complex ones if you pilot one plane and your child pilots one that is faster but leaves after yours, trying to decide when your child will overtake your plane.

If airplanes don't appeal, you might make him a checkout counter employee, having to figure costs and make change. A hungry child might want to learn to cook, using recipes to learn math and improve grades. You have a family recipe calling for fractions of cups, teaspoons, tablespoons, and other items. However, your child is an imaginary chef for a restaurant serving a banquet for 600. Have the chef take your recipe for four and change it so the 600 can be fed. Or do the reverse; figure the amounts yourself, then tell your chef that the same recipe must be cut back for two.

Perhaps your child is having trouble with languages. Now he or she is an imaginary tourist in a foreign country. A menu must be prepared for dinner and your child must select the desired item in the language of the country. Items must be identified and requests made in that language. This can be combined with math a bit by having foreign currency.

Whatever the subject, you can devise a game to match. You might also reinforce it, both before and after, through fractional relaxation. (Fractional relaxation is the relaxation process in which one relaxes all parts of the body from the toes to the top of the head, with eyes closed and the entire body rested in a comfortable position.) This time your child starts by saying, "I can learn this math (or French, Spanish, or whatever). I can do so well my teacher will be proud of me. I am going to get high grades. My studying will pay off. I can do it." Then have your child play the fantasy game and do the fractional relaxation and visualization exercise immediately afterward. This is constant, positive reinforcement.

There are several reasons why all these techniques work so effectively. One is that the child is getting positive reinforcement from you. You are working to help, praising your child's actions and spending concentrated time with your child. Children do not need constant parental attention, but they need *concentrated* attention when you *can* be with them, even if this is only for an average of ten minutes a day. It is that concentration which strengthens them emotionally and gives them the courage to try. These exercises do not take much of your time and most parents with whom I work do not find them a problem.

The fractional relaxation techniques provide a different kind of positive reinforcement. They prove to your child that he or she can learn to relax through the use of inner resources. They also change his or her thinking so that your child truly believes in the potential within, instead of carrying the typical attitude "I'll try for Mommy and Daddy but I know I can't do this." The latter is an example of personal negativism and does not help anyone.

A third reason the techniques work is that your child really does have the ability to learn. Most children and adults never learn to begin to approach their potential. This exercise helps your child reach that potential in a way that seems like a fantasy game.

Some therapists who work with children like to call the technique of using fractional relaxation before and after a fantasy game a "super" learning experience. They feel this way because your child can use this same concept to improve his or her memory. Many exceptional children have learned to train themselves to have the most effective possible study sessions by previsualization and then reinforcing themselves immediately after study the same way. Thus it is a fantasy game with tremendous potential.

Sheila's parents were frustrated by her inability to handle math. Intelligent professionals, they were convinced that Sheila had greater potential in math than she was showing. They were right, though they did not realize that they could have been of average intelligence and still have had a daughter with exceptional potential. An average child who is able to learn to use the exceptional qualities within will often surpass a genius who has not been able to tap so much of his or her potential.

I went immediately to visualization techniques with Sheila, knowing that they would work quickly and effectively. But I quickly found that Sheila was not responsive. She was old enough, at ten, to have developed a stubborn attitude. "I don't want to do what you say because it's no use. Math's too hard for me. Some kids do it and some don't. I guess I'm one of those who just can't do it. Besides, all those numbers confuse me and I can't really concentrate. I'm just not able to understand." Sheila had reached a level your child probably never will. She had a poor self-image concerning her exceptional potential.

Thus I first had to talk her through her feelings concerning her failures. "What is it that you don't understand?" I asked.

"I don't understand the reason why I should learn math. I just don't see why I should do it."

"Math is important, Sheila," I told her. "Maybe it doesn't seem like much now, but when you grow up, you'll use it a lot. Your father is active in the stock market, isn't he?"

"Yes, but that doesn't use math. It's just pieces of paper."

"He uses math to understand the changing prices. And your uncle builds bridges. He uses math to calculate how to span a river with a bridge. And your mother imports shoes. Without math she wouldn't know how to stock her stores."

Sheila could accept the general idea of using math as part of a truly exciting future career but didn't want to be bothered with learning it at the moment. However, I had excited her interest enough to convince her to try to learn some of the fantasy games.

Sheila started with the game of peace. Then she learned fractional relaxation and visualized the peace. She also fantasized sharing that peace with her mother and father.

Gradually I had Sheila share her silent peace with a broader group of people. She shared it with her brother, then her friends, and finally with her math teacher. Each time she visualized the person growing happier and feeling loving thoughts about her because of what she was doing. The people she created in her mind all smiled and were happy to be with her. Naturally she balked a bit when I brought up her math teacher but, slowly, she managed to feel happy with her visualization of the teacher, too.

Finally I had Sheila begin thinking about the math during her fractional relaxation. I had her think about the first day she ever studied it back in first grade. Then I had her think about the time since and what it was like. I had her visualize her present teacher as happy, trying to help her with the calm feeling brought by the peace Sheila had visualized.

"You know, Dr. Green, I think you are right. I think getting over the mechanics of math is not so bad when you think of all the things you can do with it." Sheila learned to use the technique of visualizing success with the math before each test. She felt better and within the next grading period, she went from a C to an A in the subject.

Eleven-year-old Jerry required more than fantasy games to help him, yet the fantasy games were an important tool. He was earning

D's in school, seldom happy, often having mood swings, and generally feeling himself out of place with everything and everyone. He hated school, and his parents rightfully feared he might mark time in class until he was old enough to quit.

The first discovery I made was that Jerry's diet was heavily composed of nonnutritious, heavily sugared food. When he did well, his parents would reward him with a chocolate bar or take him for french fries and ice cream which he dearly loved. They noticed his mood swing an hour or so later, when he was unable to settle down to study. They blamed his agitation on adolescence. When I showed them diet alternatives, they tried them and Jerry responded immediately. His mood shifts ended. He became calm, self-controlled, and was no longer depressed. He stopped having difficulty concentrating and liked himself better.

Next I began working with Jerry using fantasy games related to school. I had him practice fractional relaxation while visualizing himself doing well in school. I had him think of being happy and successful, getting good grades and being friends with both the other students and teachers. As he developed this positive attitude, he was able to work to full capacity. His grades, which had been D in almost everything, suddenly went to the top; in fact, his teachers at first thought he must be cheating because the change was so sudden. He wasn't cheating, he had just used fantasy games to turn around his negative attitude and help him tap his exceptional qualities.

The older child, even an exceptional one, may be having trouble in school because of boredom. A child will sometimes excel in something, lose interest in other areas, then get told by parents and teachers that he or she has to spend more time working on the less favored subjects. The child stops trying altogether since he or she is not encouraged in the field where there is already maximum performance.

You should always accentuate your child's strong points to give your child the self-respect needed to learn to overcome his or her weak points. When you draw too much attention to the negative in your child's life, your child begins to feel stupid. Eventually grades suffer and even you will likely feel that the weaker grades reflect your child's abilities. The process becomes self-perpetuatingly destructive.

If you have an older child, there is a chance that your child needs a change in self-image in order to bring forth the exceptional qualities. Fortunately you can use fantasy games to do this quickly and effectively. Remember that you were no different from any other parent when you first picked up this book. You probably made some mistakes.

Andrea was typical of the older child whose parents loved and cared about her mental and emotional growth, but who were inadvertently never giving her credit. Her parents were perfectionists. When she brought home compositions full of ideas well in advance of her years, they ignored the brilliance of her reasoning and acted as editors. They were so busy crossing "t's," dotting "i's," and correcting spelling, they never really paid attention to what their daughter was trying to say.

Next Andrea turned to chemistry. She had a chemistry set she wanted to use for experimentation well beyond the projects in the instruction book. Instead of encouraging this creative action, her parents said she shouldn't do it for fear she would blow up the house. Even Andrea's grades were a problem. If she got a B+, her father told her she should be getting an A. Only the best was good enough and Andrea came to feel that even her best might be criticized.

When Andrea entered my office, she seemed defeated. She was a ten-year-old blue-eyed blond with a brilliant mind. She talked about how she had once loved learning to read and write, despite the fact that she was now having trouble passing English grammar and composition. She said she wasn't interested in the subjects any more.

"I find it boring," Andrea said, "I don't like it. It is all so boring for me."

"Is it boring because you don't like the teacher?"

"Yes, I like the teacher."

"Then maybe it would help if you tried a fantasy game other children seem to like," I told her. Unfortunately she said she was so bored with English grammar and composition that it wasn't worth trying my game. That would be boring, too.

I decided to try a slight variation. There are experiences in life which trigger an emotional response that is the most intense we can have. These are positive and often overwhelm us so slowly and quietly that we do not realize until they are over how profoundly they have moved our emotions. I am not speaking of violence or death or great romance. These would not be common to children. Instead I am speaking of seeing a sunset from the side of a hill, perhaps being at the beach as the sun bakes our bodies and the surf washes us as we lie near the edge of the shore, or some other pleasant experience. For a child, it might have taken place on vacation or, surprising for the parents, it might be as simple as a time sitting on Daddy's or Mommy's lap while reading a book aloud.

Each such experience is deeply moving. It is something an adult can share with a child.

"Andrea," I said, "I want to try a game that doesn't relate to school. I want you to sit so you're comfortable, perhaps close your eyes and not really think about much of anything. Don't try to concentrate on anything except my voice and the question I'm going to ask you.

"I want you to think back in your past, Andrea. I want you to think of a time when you felt really happy. I want you to think of a time when you thought life was really wonderful. I want you to think of the happiest time you can remember, when everything felt perfect, you were happy, and felt terrific. Can you do that?"

A smile crossed Andrea's face. "Oh, yes, Dr. Green. I can remember when my Mommy and Daddy took me to the beach. I went to the water and it was so calm. It was the sea but it was like a swimming pool. It was so warm and there were palm trees everywhere. It was in Florida and we went to Disney World after that. I saw Mickey Mouse. It was just a wonderful time. I remember it so well."

"All right, now, Andrea, I want you to keep your eyes closed and remember in your imagination what it was like. I want you to see yourself on the beach in Miami. I want you to feel the warm water and the sun. I want you to smell the trees and all the aromas of the day. And I want you to take yourself back to Disney World, to seeing Donald Duck and Mickey Mouse and all the others. Just experience the feelings, the excitement, and the joy you felt then. Take your time. Focus on the best moments and relive them in your mind as though they were happening now. Remember how you felt, the meaning it had for you." I paused, then added, "Now tell me what you are feeling that is so good."

"The sea," she said, softly. "I'm swimming in the sea with my brother. Everything is so different from a pool. There's no chlorine to sting my eyes. And it's so easy to move about. I love it, Dr. Green.

"And Disney World," she continued, laughing slightly, "all the rides and the people and Mickey Mouse."

"Now, Andrea, I want you to take this a step further. I want you to retain those memories and that feeling of happiness but now I want you to transport yourself to a high mountain. The sun is shining overhead. It is warm and you feel very much at peace, just as you did that time in Florida." I was giving Andrea an exercise which is common to a therapy concept called psychosynthesis. It is a way of reaching that part of everyone's mind, including children, which helps guide us to further understanding of our lives.

"Now while you are on this mountain, I want you to visualize a ray of light coming from the sun and shining on the ground next to where you are standing. As you look closely, you will see an old man in the light. He is a wise old man who deeply loves you. He is gentle and kind and the smartest person you have ever met. You can see by looking in his eyes that he deeply loves you even though this is the first time you have seen him.

"As you watch this warm sunbeam, the wise old man begins to step out. He is standing next to you, your friend, someone you can confide in and share with and he'll understand. I want you to tell this wise old man about going to the beach and to Disney World."

There was a pause, then Andrea said, "He thinks it was wonderful, too."

"I want you to ask the wise old man how you can make that feeling a part of your life. I want you to be able to feel as relaxed and happy as you did in Florida, right here where you live. I want you to remember some of the things you did which helped make it so good."

Andrea thought hard for a minute, then said, "I was very happy then and nobody scolded me. I was nice with my brother and he was nice with me. I remember thinking how nice it would be if we could share those feelings all the time."

"What do you mean when you say that you were nice to your brother?"

"You know. Nice with him. I looked after him because he's my younger brother and he was very little at the time. I helped him swim in the water and I held his hand when we went through Disney World. I had to show him Mickey Mouse and he wasn't scared when I did that. I felt so happy myself that I didn't mind helping my brother. I think I liked it and it made me feel so good."

"You weren't bored in Florida, were you, Andrea?"

"Oh, no, everything was so wonderful."

"That sounds like a really happy time, Andrea. Now I want you to continue feeling the way you did in Florida, then move ahead in your mind to the present time. I want you to keep feeling this happiness and excitement, only now, instead of being at the beach, you are seeing yourself doing the English grammar and composition you once thought were boring. This time, as you see yourself working the problems the teacher is giving you, you feel what you felt in Florida. You feel happy and excited and not at all bored. And when you have any questions, any difficulties you can't handle, you have the wise old man standing next to you. You can ask him questions and he'll get you through the difficulties."

Andrea kept smiling. "That's wonderful, Dr. Green. I don't like being bored. I guess if I could really feel this way when doing my English, I wouldn't be bored. I'd be happy about it. And maybe I'd be happier with my family again. I'm not very nice to my brother right now because I'm not always very happy. But I know my brother loves me. I remember how he was in Florida and I know I should be nice to him because I like myself when I am."

"Now Andrea, while you've got these good feelings inside, I want you to think about something. I want you to answer a question and you can ask the wise old man if you aren't sure what would be best. I want you to think about that experience you enjoyed and what you could do in your English class to begin feeling the same way."

"I guess I could be nicer to the people in the class. I could be nicer to my teacher, too. It's like my brother. I never liked him very much until we were in Florida and I got all excited about Mickey Mouse and Donald Duck. I felt so good and I began seeing him differently. Maybe if I'm nicer to my teacher and the other kids in my class, I'll see English differently. Maybe I'll like it at least a little bit. Maybe it won't be so boring if I do that."

"All right, now I want you to try that with your English. You've been feeling so good you know you can try it. When do you want to start?"

"Tomorrow. I have a class tomorrow."

"That's a great idea, Andrea," I told her. "I want you to make a pact with yourself that you will do just that. You've said that you will do it and you've felt those good feelings already. I want you to tell yourself that tomorrow you really will try this in your class and see if maybe the work isn't boring anymore."

Finally I had Andrea finish with the fantasy exercise of visualizing herself doing English composition, getting an A, feeling happy, and having the friendly teacher and other students gather around her to congratulate her. She was to bring this image into herself, making it a part of herself. She repeated this with similar images above, below, and all around her. It was the same approach I discussed before.

During the next weeks, Andrea started feeling better about herself. She was more happy and relaxed.

I said, "If you try what we've been talking about, I think we'll all be very happy."

Andrea did enjoy the class. She didn't feel the same excitement she had in Disney World, but she did feel at peace. She was relaxed, comfortable with others, and happy about the learning. She realized that the work could be a challenge and it was a challenge she enjoyed trying to meet. She liked the work and she liked herself. She even started helping others who had difficulty with their compositions during their free periods when the students had a chance to work on their homework.

I also spoke with Andrea's parents. They began to realize that they had not given Andrea credit for her ten-year-old accomplishments. They had been so busy looking only at her flaws that they had stopped seeing how special she was.

A few weeks later, Andrea's teacher called me. She had just finished talking with Andrea's mother and her mother wanted me to hear the information first hand. "I don't know what happened," said the teacher. "Andrea's changed. She used to be so sullen and withdrawn, and now she's excited about the class work. She never was before, and she's . . . it's hard to say this about a student but . . . she's really much nicer than before. All of a sudden, she's like a different child. I never really noticed her though I don't like to say that about a student. It's just . . . Well, the important thing is I'm finding her delightful to have in my class. She's so helpful, a real leader, and her enjoyment is infectious. It's really making a difference."

Andrea's grades went up as well. Her exceptional brilliance was showing now. Both her regular work and her extracurricular compositions were earning top awards. She went from being an average student who never really worked to one who was at the top of her class. It all started with the fantasy game.

For children under seven, sometimes you will want to use a fantasy game that reinforces the real world by creating a nonsense world which your child unconsciously uses for comparison, a game which stretches your child's imagination and can be extremely stimulating for his or her creative abilities. Here's an example:

The idea behind this game is to create a fantasy image that is impossible. You say, "I can't think of anything sillier than seeing a zebra playing a guitar in a rock group." Or you can create any other image you want. Then you have your child say, "I can't think of anything sillier than . . ." Your child completes this statement, perhaps saying: ". . . than a banana driving a school bus." And so it goes. You each trade off, coming up with nonsense phrases. It is a simple word game but it teaches creativity, imagination, language, and other essential aspects of being exceptional.

Another word game is effective for your young children. This is one which allows for rhyming words. You might try words that rhyme with "like" such as "bike," "mike," "trike," and so forth. Or "love," "dove," "shove," adding until you have to quit. You alternate choosing words and then rhyming them.

All these fantasy games can be changed and adapted to your needs. They give you a chance to enter into the world of imagination with your child. You learn to appreciate a child's special inner world. At the same time, your child becomes exceptional in ways that do not seem like dull learning experiences for him or her. This is important for your child's growth.

Now on to a more structured form of fantasy games.

5

Pressing Your Child's Magic Button

If there ever was a magic button to help your child be in touch with himself, it is meditation. All human beings are capable of meditation. It's normal, easy, and pleasurable. The word comes from the Sanskrit word "medha" meaning wisdom. It leads to wisdom because it gives the brain enough quiet to focus and center on nothing. Only when the mind is completely undistracted is it able to retrieve, like a computer, from the data bank of all the sensations and knowledge in our brain. This enables us to come up with answers and insights that our ordinary waking consciousness would never allow us to do.

What can meditation do for your child?

1. Increase the child's ability to concentrate.
2. Help the child to sustain his attention, lengthen attention span.
3. Help the child to become more in harmony with himself therefore increasing self-confidence.
4. Dispel negative thoughts and fantasies.

Meditation will enhance your child's creative imagination by putting him in touch with the wide range of associations, memories, and ideas he possesses but has forgotten.

The next level of meditation opens up your child to the intuitive. Intuition is the act of knowing without using the rational process. If you meditate after information has been synthesized, juxtaposition of various parts allow the truly original insight or "eureka." Einstein said that major advances in science owe much to intuition and to "being sympathetically in touch with experience." Einstein said that he came to intuition by continuing to ask himself questions about space and time that only children ask.

At what age can your child be involved with meditation? Virtually before birth. Expectant mothers who meditate can feel the fetus relaxing in their womb. Some mothers try to communicate their love for their unborn infants by imagining love as a ray of light, warm and enveloping. This exercise can be done when the fetus is kicking and causing discomfort or any time the mother wants to make contact. The emotional and mental state of the mother is transferred to the fetus just as food and drink are carried through her bloodstream to nourish the placenta. The symbiosis is both mental and physical.

Some children will be able to start using visualization techniques the first time they try meditation. Others need to be introduced slowly to the experience.

One way to introduce imagery to your child is to tell him or her to identify with a wave in the sea. "Your wave slowly rises and falls, rises and falls," you might say. "Each time you breathe in, the wave slowly rises. As you exhale, the sea relaxes and the wave flattens. Inhale, with your wave rising; exhale and the wave flattens. Up and down. Isn't it nice to be a wave moving across the sea? In and out. Up and down. Each time you breathe, the wave moves gently through the water."

There is a connection between the higher brain waves and certain rhythms in nature. This is why looking at the waves of the ocean is so conducive to relaxation. For this same reason, when you have a fireplace and watch the flames of the fire, the experience is hypnotic.

Once your child is enjoying the experience of being a wave, have him tense his or her body. "Make a fist and tense all the muscles in your legs, your feet, and your arms. Tense your face, your mouth, and nose. Sit straight up, your whole body is tense now, as it had been relaxed. Get as tense as you can.

"Now let all that tense energy out. You are like a blown-up balloon with all the air rushing out. You are as relaxed as the balloon is soft and limp. There isn't a drop of tension in your body. You are sitting straight but completely relaxed.

"Now keep your eyes closed and look inside yourself. Imagine you see a spot inside your head, right between your eyebrows. It is a spot right in the center of your forehead. Can you see it?

"Now instead of looking at the spot, I want you to try and feel as though you *are* that spot. You are standing in the center of yourself. You can feel yourself on the spot in the middle of your forehead.

"Now feel as if there is a shining light inside of you. This light is right in the center of your forehead. You and that light are the same. You are becoming that light. Can you feel yourself being that light in the middle of your forehead? It is very comfortable for you. You feel very relaxed and happy. You are a warm, comfortable ray of light right in the middle of your forehead."

Most children respond to this approach. You can change the language as necessary so your child understands the image being created. You will be able to see your child relax and enjoy the fantasy image.

Some children do not immediately relax because their minds remain filled with thoughts of the television program, game, or other activity with which they were most recently involved. This is normal and there is a simple way to handle this difficulty.

Once your child has done the tensing and relaxing, tell your child to be the wave again. "Each time your wave rises and falls, you will go deeper into meditation, deeper into relaxation. I will count the waves, and when I reach ten, you will be the quietest wave in the calmest sea you can imagine. You will be deeply relaxed. You will be more relaxed than you have ever been before. You will be quiet, calm, and relaxed."

If there is still some restlessness, repeat this approach while having your child lie on his or her back. Your child may fall asleep the first few times and this is fine. Once your child is comfortable with this approach, you will find that he or she is able to begin meditation more quickly.

After your child has learned to concentrate the light beam, your child is ready to try a more advanced level of meditation. This is the merging of a human feeling with an image. To do this, your child looks inward at the center of his or her forehead. There is an imaginary dot in the middle of the circle.

"Do you see the dot? It is right in the center of the circle. Now imagine that you are the dot and the circle is the entire world.

"What color is your dot? What color is the circle? That's very good.

"Now I want you to be very quiet, very still, as you look at this beautiful dot within the circle. I want you to imagine love. I want this love to be right inside your dot, completely filling it.

"Now give your dot more love. Give your dot so much love that it can not handle it all without growing larger and larger. The more you love, the bigger the dot will grow.

"Reach into your heart for love. Feel your love flowing from your heart into the dot. You are giving that dot more and more of your heart's love. You are feeling quiet, relaxed, at peace with the love flowing into that dot.

"Now the dot is reaching the edge of the circle. The dot and the circle are one. You and the world are one. Your love has made you as big as the world.

"Take a look at this wonderful dot, so big and filled with love. What color is your dot? What color is your circle? What color have they become now that they are all one?

"Did you know that the real world is just like this? Instead of being the only dot in the world, there are many dots and they all can grow together with love. The more you love, the more you grow and mix with all the other dots until your love and the world are one and everyone is so happy. Your love is making the world very happy. You feel good about this, don't you? Love is such a nice feeling, isn't it?"

This kind of exercise is best started around age five, the time your child is able to visualize an emotion and sustain the image.

Many of us don't understand the distinctions among daydreaming, fantasy, and meditation. Daydreaming and fantasy are the child's earliest escapes from everyday reality, unguided and playful, whereas meditation is guided and purposeful. It is important not to criticize your child's lapses into daydreams. Instead, understand that this is your child's spontaneous way of getting within the mind, the very facility you will be encouraging in meditation.

How do you, as a parent, become skilled in getting your child into meditation? It's easy if you follow these four guidelines. First, give her a quiet environment. Meditation can be achieved in any quiet location. At first you want a location that is familiar and comfortable for your child, such as a family room or the bedroom. You can anticipate that your children will be thinking of a television program they want to watch or a game they want to play. Thus you should first ask them to empty their minds as best they can, just observing any thoughts as passing clouds. External distractions can also be anticipated. You might want to take the phone off the hook and put a "do not disturb" sign on the door.

Second, give him an idea, concept, or object to dwell on. This can be the effort of relaxing different parts of the body. You can also have your child think of a word or repeating sounds. I find children most receptive to the idea of trying to relax various parts of their body.

Third, help her assume a passive attitude, which means emptying all thoughts from the mind. Learning to let go of thoughts and succumb to the meditation is the most important ingredient.

Fourth, make sure your children are in a comfortable position. Their arms and legs should not be crossed and they should not have on confining clothing. Loosen collars and belts if necessary.

You may be concerned about your child's learning to meditate because you still feel a sense of discomfort that you are asking your child to do something strange. However meditation is a natural human function. Everyone meditates in some way, though usually it is unguided. You are teaching your child to meditate in a manner which will help develop exceptional qualities.

Children like a schedule. They can be defiant when you force them to vary what they perceive to be a comfortable routine. They will be more receptive to learning meditation if you can establish a time of day when your entire family can sit down and meditate together.

At first you only want your child to learn to relax. Children constantly run around, then suddenly drop from exhaustion. They sleep deeply, then get up to run around all over again. You are introducing an activity that brings a gentle serenity to your child during time usually devoted to intense physical activity. Just learning to slow the process of mind and body enough to relax is an excellent first step toward mastering meditation.

There are many ways to start the meditation process. One way is to let your child imitate your actions as I did with my son when I played the game of giving him peace. Even children as young as two will close their eyes and slow their breathing in imitation of their parents. This can be a good game for a young child though it works with older children as well.

Another approach is to start by teaching your child to focus his or her attention. For example, take your child to a garden, an approach used with Linda whose mother took her to see me. Eight-year-old Linda was having difficulty focusing her attention on anything for very long. Her mother was concerned when this problem made learning difficult. When she brought her to me, I took Linda to a garden to look at all the flowers, something she enjoyed doing.

"Now look at just one flower, Linda. You can pick any one that seems pretty to you. Go up to it and look at it."

Linda chose a red rose, carefully holding the stem so she would not prick her finger. She looked at it for a moment, then turned away.

"I'll bet you didn't see it, Linda," I said to her.

"I saw the flower. It was pretty."

"But did you see everything?" I asked. She looked at me quizzically.

"Take a close look at the flower. Can you see how there are dozens of little petals very close together?"

Linda looked and this time she paid more attention. She turned the flower all about, then traced the petals with her finger.

"They're all separate but they're all attached to make the flower. Look inside. Do you see the different parts of the flower?" I began naming them and pointing them out to her. She was fascinated. She had looked at the flower before but never really seen it.

"What about the others?" she asked.

"Why don't you find out."

Linda picked a different flower and compared it with the rose. She began going from flower to flower, studying each one, then carefully comparing them with the others. She was fascinated. The garden had been a blur of color and pretty forms. Then she had learned to look at one rose, isolating it from the rest of the plants. Finally she could see each flower as a unique creation. Even when she compared one rose with another, she could point out variations in color, petal design, and other aspects.

Next I had Linda focus on a bee that was going from flower to flower, gathering pollen. She watched how it buzzed the flowers, selecting one and going into it. She saw the way the pollen seemed to flake off the legs as the bee, almost overburdened with its load, flew back to its hive.

Each observation was a focusing of Linda's mind. She was narrowing her attention in order to see more than ever before. By concentrating, she was also growing in knowledge. It was a major step forward, yet to Linda, it was fun. Her mother saw that Linda applied this concept to her observations many times during each day. Linda was seeing what she had never seen before and loving every moment of the experience.

When Linda returned to my office, she was ready to learn to meditate. She then went back to school, better equipped for education. Each night her parents had a meditation session with her, as well as showing her new objects to study with the intensity she had shown the flowers. Her school grades improved and she increased her attention span to the point where it was actually better than the other students in her class.

Yet another approach is to teach proper breathing. Have your child relax and close his or her eyes. Then tell your child to inhale slowly through the nose, filling the lungs while you count slowly to four. Have your child exhale through the mouth, again using the four count. Inhale slowly through the nose; exhale slowly through the mouth. Inhale . . . Exhale . . .

Notice how your child relaxes when doing this breathing exercise. Again your child is focusing attention and learning to concentrate. Your child's only thought is on the breathing.

Once your child enjoys the preliminary techniques, it is time to start the meditation methods. Have him relax, concentrating on breathing for a few moments. Then quietly tell your child to relax his or her toes.

"Think about your toes relaxing. You know how, when you are playing, your toes sometimes hurt a bit. Think about them going to sleep. They are resting and going to sleep. They feel so good. They feel so nice.

"And your feet. They're relaxing, too. You know how when you've been running and running and you finally sit down and take off your shoes, your feet feel so good. And now they're relaxing. Your toes . . . Your feet . . . Your ankles . . .

"Your ankles are relaxing. They feel so relaxed. You're breathing in and out, slowly . . . slowly . . . and your toes, your feet, and your ankles feel so good.

"Now that relaxing feeling is spreading to your lower legs. It is going to your knees and your upper legs. You are relaxing. You feel so good. So happy. You are drifting on a cloud up in the sky. Your whole body is relaxing because that cloud is so soft. You are being held more comfortably than Mommy or Daddy could ever hold you. You are floating, your stomach and your chest relaxing. Your arms feel so good. Just floating.

"Your neck is relaxing. The cloud is like the softest pillow you can feel and it is supporting your head. Your neck feels so good, and now your chin feels relaxed. Your chin and your forehead and the very top of your head.

"You feel so relaxed from the toes of your feet to the top of your head. Isn't it wonderful? You're not worried about anything. You feel better than you've ever felt before. You are so happy and comfortable and filled with love. You're all relaxed, floating . . ."

Each time you mention a part of the body, you can lightly touch it if that seems to help your child concentrate. What you say and how long you go on talking will vary with the child's age and how long her attention span might be. What is important is getting your child to relax, if only for a few minutes.

Repeat this same exercise until your child is truly comfortable with it. Don't worry if he goes to sleep in the beginning. Most adults occasionally fall asleep when they first learn to meditate. All this means is that your child is fully relaxing. After a few days, she will be able to meditate effectively. If this is not the case you are probably having the meditation take place too close to when your child really needs sleep. Changing the hour will alleviate this problem.

After a week or two, let your child relax with you observing. She does not have to say anything aloud. You can tell by the way your child moves whether a meditative state has been reached. If it hasn't, you may have to start over, this time guiding her.

As your child relaxes, there are changes in the brain wave patterns which will affect your child's ability to realize his or her potential. All of us experience those changes if we meditate. They can be carefully charted with scientific instruments and have been known for some time. However, few parents ever learn to help their children tap these exceptional qualities.

One wave is the delta wave. This is called the unconscious wave because your brain is in delta when you are deeply sleeping.

Next comes the beta wave. This is the brain wave of mental activity. It is the wave you are experiencing at this very moment. You have the beta wave when you read, figure numbers, or engage in activities which call upon your senses. You can experience the beta wave when you are eating, talking, and thinking. Your child was experiencing the beta wave when you did the attention focusing exercise. Looking at the flower caused your child to tap the senses of sight and smell. If your child is very young, probably taste was experienced as well.

The alpha wave is the key to creativity. When you help your child achieve the alpha wave, you have unleashed creativity and personal growth. By making suggestions to your child when he or she is experiencing the alpha wave, you can strongly influence your child's development. Your child is going to be experiencing the alpha wave when relaxation is complete. It is a wave he or she may reach just before falling asleep or while daydreaming. However, at such times it is not being guided in a way that can increase your child's ability to reach full personal potential. This is what you will do now.

The theta wave is a step beyond alpha. Theta waves indicate a mental state that can lead to what is considered an altered state of consciousness. Theta waves are involved when experiencing paranormal phenomena, such as ESP, clairvoyance, telepathy.

Never be concerned with whether or not your child is actually in the alpha state when you do these exercises. Some children reach alpha for but a brief second or two. Others are in the state for several minutes. Each time your child meditates, the ability to tap into the alpha state will grow.

There is a technique which can be used with your child when he or she is in a meditative state—visualization. Visualization is the forming of your goal into a mental picture. Visualization is a precondition of realizing any thought or action.

If your child is in a meditative state, it is possible to improve his or her self-image, thus improving the ability to learn. This exercise also brings you closer together. It is a beautiful form of communication between parent and child. Ask yourself what changes you want to bring forth? With a very small child, you might want to work on the aptitude for giving, sharing, loving, and friendship.

Start by talking with your child about the characteristic you want to develop. For example, suppose you would like to increase your child's compassion. Talk with your child about what happens when he or she sees someone get hurt. Use situations with which your child can identify, such as a friend falling on the pavement while trying to roller skate. Get your child to think how he or she would feel in the same situation. Guide your child into an awareness of how he or she would need comfort and sympathy with such a fall, then would feel contentment when it is received.

Make a game of it. Create a situation to which your child can relate, such as running across the ground and having a friend fall over a rock. Talk about how your child could react.

Next have your child visualize using the relaxation method.

You can teach your child to share, to love a new baby brother or sister, or do anything else that helps develop exceptional qualities of compassion, love, and similar values. These are quite general, but ideal for small children.

The older the child, the more you can vary and refine your use of visualization. For example, suppose your child is having trouble learning a foreign language. You might have your child fantasize studying. Then he is mentally going to school, taking a test, and answering the questions correctly and easily. Or she might fantasize talking with someone from the country whose language he or she is trying to learn. In the fantasy, the two children are speaking fluently. Naturally, to reinforce the learning process you will always start with the idea of your child studying hard at first. You will always end with your child being very happy and everyone around him—you, your spouse, the teacher, the classmate—being very happy as well.

The older child should take all this a step further through visualization discussed earlier. The image you want him to experience, such as doing well in school, is first imagined as being physically in front of him, then pulled into the body to make it a part of him. Next it is imagined to the left, to the right, above, and below. Each time, the wording is repeated, and your child makes the mental image come inside, combining the fantasy with the physical body.

The visualization techniques, once mastered, can be a tool to get over any rough periods. Your school-age child can easily turn to them just before a big test, the presentation of a paper before the class, or before an athletic event, as well as changing attitudes toward learning, friends, parents, teachers, and others.

You are the best judge of the time when your child should be able to visualize an emotion and hold the image. You will also be modifying the approach according to their age.

There are a number of ways to increase the ability to visualize in order to stimulate the latent creative abilities. Remember that every child can increase the limits of these creative abilities. Some scientists say that the average person uses only ten percent of his brain. Naturally this is just conjecture since no one knows what it would mean to use one hundred percent of our abilities. However, it does illustrate the fact that we can learn to use more of our mind than we do.

Not every child can be turned into a genius, capable of making discoveries which will revolutionize the world. What you want is to develop your child's ability to tap his or her full potential. Learning to concentrate and use meditation for a positive self-image will result in being able to absorb more information. He or she will become a superior student, able to achieve full mental capacity.

As the older child progresses with visualization, the techniques can be adapted to expand self-awareness. Here are two examples:

Have your child imagine a tall building. "You are standing at the top of this tall building and there is a winding staircase going down to the ground. Can you see this staircase? It is long and wide and easy to walk on. You are going to be able to get down easily.

"Now put your foot on the first step and start going downstairs. Every ten steps the staircase turns a corner. See how it is as you are going down the first step, the second, the third . . ." You keep counting through the tenth.

"Now turn the corner and you will start down some more. One, two, three, four. . . ." You keep talking, watching your child relax. You might stop with this level or you might take your child down another landing or two in his or her imaginary journey.

"Now we're at the bottom of the staircase and you can see a trapdoor. Open the trapdoor and look inside. You can see that this leads directly inside yourself. But this trapdoor does not reach into just any place. It leads to that part of yourself where the right answer for every problem exists.

"Now walk through the trapdoor and step inside. Ask yourself a question about something that is bothering you. Don't ask out loud. Ask inside, talking only to yourself.

"Notice how the answer comes? Maybe it won't come in so many words, but you will know the right way to go, the right things to do. The answer is real."

After a few moments, you continue:

"Now try to feel your toes. Keep your eyes closed and just try to sense your toes.

"Imagine your toes are vanishing into air. Then feel your feet as they, too, become lighter and lighter, also vanishing into the air. Your ankles disappear and then your legs, your body, your arms, and your head. What is left is yourself, that inner awareness of everything in your life. It is inside your body, yet separate from your body, so it does not need your body to survive.

"Suddenly your body returns. You can again feel your toes, your feet, your ankles, your legs, and the rest of your body. You can sense taste on your tongue, hear your breathing, and feel your muscles all restored. Now open your eyes and look around."

Another exercise for older children is to imagine that there is a rocket ship in their head. Again, this is done after the child is relaxed.

"Step inside your rocket ship. It is docked right in the center of your head so it is easy to get inside.

"What color is your rocket ship? Can you feel it take off and start to travel all the way to the top of your head?

"Now that rocket ship, carrying you inside, has left the limits of your head and is going out into space. You can look out the window in the rocket ship and see yourself travel past all the planets and the stars. You are moving so fast and passing so many planets and stars that it is impossible for you to count them all. There are millions of them all around you.

"Now your rocket ship is descending. You are going back past the planets and stars. You are coming through the earth's atmosphere but there is nothing to fear. Your rocket ship can handle any problems without any risk.

"Your rocket ship has touched the ground and now is slicing through, going down into the earth. It is in the center and passing through to the other side. Now it is going up through the atmosphere again, this time going higher and higher into space, reaching farther into space than ever before.

"Your ship is coming back now. Soaring past planets and stars with you happily inside. See up ahead of you? There is a space station which you are circling.

"Now you are returning to your head. Your rocket ship is reentering your head just as it left before. It is back inside, back into the center where you first got on board. It has slowed and now is coming to a complete stop, smoothly, without jarring your head or yourself.

"Step out of your rocket ship. It has just taken you on a tour of the universe. You have been everywhere you can possibly go in space.

"What did you see in your universe? What did you experience during your travels through space? What did you experience inside your own awareness within your head?" Ask your child about this experience and it will come alive even more in his or her mind.

A meditation that will help a child feel in harmony with the universe can be done outside. Take her outdoors on a sunny day. Sit comfortably on the ground and look at the grass. Have her concentrate on the grass while relaxing. You may have to have your child try the slow breathing technique at first, but most children will relax automatically on a pleasant day, sitting in the sun, and staring at the grass.

Have her imagine that she is becoming a blade of grass. "Feel what it is like to be green and growing in the ground. Feel the wind as it gently blows you. Feel what it is like to live in harmony with all the other blades of grass. The blade is unique and yet it is one among many, living in peace just as you are happy living in peace with others in the world. Try to feel this oneness with everyone around you, just as the blade of grass is one with the lawn."

These are the many ways you can help your child meditate and work with guided imagery. You can also create your own visualizations and help your child create his or hers.

Meditation increases concentration, quality of thought, as well as being a means for your child to develop inspired and original thought. Studies of geniuses and artists show that they have used meditation and visualization to tap into their brains, thus giving the world unique contributions.

Because meditation is the key to creativity, it is important to take time to practice the concepts in this chapter. You will see a dramatic change in learning ability and perceptions, and you will help your child tap the full abilities of his or her mind.

6

It's Better to Give than to Receive, but Try to Tell a Two-year-old

As immature as young children are, they are capable of levels of compassion and understanding that we come to expect only in maturity.

Among the most desirable qualities in every human are the abilities to have compassion and give to others. Such individuals make the best leaders, whether doctors or corporate executives. By being sensitive to those around them and understanding the needs of others, they can learn to deal effectively with any situation. They will know how to manage through positive motivation and to administer in a way that instills the loyalty and respect of those under them.

Altruism is the quality of taking an action because you are concerned about the welfare of someone else. It is a quality found in more mature, emotionally developed individuals. It is generally believed that the less mature a person, the more self-involved that individual behaves. Such a person has difficulty being sensitive to the needs of others. However, recent clinical studies with children have proven that even the very young have innate feelings of compassion and altruism. These can be developed in all children, including your own.

Let's take a look at two theories of childhood concerning compassion and giving. One is that children are self-centered, greedy, and vicious toward one another until they are taught otherwise. Battles over toys are seen as mini-wars fought by tiny combatants who will stop at nothing in order to triumph. The small child is seen as someone who takes all and gives nothing. The second view is that children are good, kind, pure, and innocent until corrupted by the cruel world around them. A small child naturally wants to share everything he or she has.

Neither extreme is the case. Children are naturally altruistic, but also vulnerable. They see the love of an adult as something they can easily lose. The fear of this loss makes them act in a selfish manner to try and protect their needs. Yet when they do not feel this threat, they are loving, sharing human beings whose natural instincts are to care about others.

For example, two small children are out playing on a slide. They are good friends, having a grand time, when one of them falls, hits the ground, and skins his knee. He begins to cry and a parent comes rushing over. As the injured child receives all the attention, the other child suddenly develops an imaginary injury and walks around demanding "Kiss my boo-boo." He will not behave until he too has been checked for injury.

The parent knows that the injured child is the one in need of attention, not his or her own, unhurt child. The fact that their child seems to be demanding attention makes the child seem selfish.

A small child thinks that if his parent's concern is related to someone else, he may be in jeopardy of permanently losing the parent's affection. Remember when I discussed the game of peek-a-boo? I said that what delights a child is the affirmation that disappearing objects are not gone forever just because they cannot be seen. A baby sees the world as either existing or not existing. If something is present, then it is real. The child applies the peek-a-boo objects to loved ones who "disappear" but still come back.

Small children view punishment similarly. If your child plays with a toy that is forbidden in the house, such as a large ball, and knocks over an heirloom lamp, she is going to be punished. Not only have you been disobeyed, the consequence you feared most has resulted.

Yet the child sees more than this. He may decide that you do not love him at all.

Children do not have the maturity to understand that discipline is a regular part of a loving relationship. To them, a relationship with a parent is often either all love or no love. The child does not see anything else until taught to understand that love is not withdrawn just because one action is being punished.

The child who demands attention is not selfish. He's saying, "If Mommy is helping Suzie with her knee, then Mommy doesn't care about me. Mommy only loves Suzie, and if I don't get Mommy's attention, she won't want me to be her child anymore."

Your child's conscious thinking is not that sophisticated, of course. If you talk with your child about why he is pretending to have an injury, he might deny there is any fantasy involved, or he might say, "I don't know." However, you, the parent, can deal with this situation very easily.

First, don't get angry. It doesn't matter whether the injury to the other child is a skinned knee or a broken arm. The seriousness of the problem is beyond your child's comprehension. Your child's initial concern is the possibility of losing you.

One answer is to have your child help. "Suzie hurt herself, Johnny. Why don't we see if we can help her? She is in pain. It would really be wonderful of you because you remember how much you wanted someone to help you the last time you were hurt. We can work together to make her feel better."

You can use other approaches as well. The important point is that you let your child feel that by acting more maturely, he or she is going to be winning your pleasure, love, and approval.

Once the emergency care has been provided, you should sit with the other children and reinforce the altruistic act. "I'm very proud of the way you helped Suzie. You'd like Suzie to help me comfort you if you had gotten hurt and not her. That's why it was so good of you to help her when she was injured."

Naturally what you say and how you say it will depend upon the way you usually speak and the age of the child. Only the message remains consistent: When you help someone else, you are doing something that is very good for everyone.

Another common problem area is with the sharing of toys. All human beings have possessive instincts. We establish a sense of identity, in part, from what we own. This might be a home, a car, a collection of stamps, or almost anything else. I am most comfortable with the familiar surroundings of my office when I am at work. Some families see a kitchen table as their most important possession because they remember childhood experiences of happy times talking while sitting around the table. A writer may value a typewriter, a photographer a favorite camera.

Children are no different. A toy truck or a doll provides your child with a sense of identity. The item has much greater importance than adults generally think. When a child refuses to share the toy, it is because he or she does not want to lose this sense of identity.

You should never get mad at a child who refuses to share a toy. Instead, it is important to explain two points to your child. The first is that the toy will not be taken. "Larry isn't going to keep your truck. Larry is going to play with your truck while he's here, just as you play with Larry's train when you're at his house. Larry will give it back before he leaves."

The second point is that sharing toys ensures that the friend will return. "It won't be any fun for Larry to come here if he has nothing to play with. If you want Larry to play with you, then you have to share your toys. You wouldn't want to go over to Larry's house if he didn't let you play with the toys he has. Why should Larry want to come over here if you don't share with him? You can either have the pleasure of Larry's company or you can play with your toys all by yourself. I think it is much nicer to have Larry over to play, even though it means sharing, than to be the only person allowed to play with your toys and never have a friend who wants to come here, don't you?"

Again the exact wording will vary with what is effective for your child. What is important is that you are showing your child that the only alternative to sharing is isolation from friends. There is no punishment. You are giving him real alternatives. However, by letting your child make the choice instead of telling her what to do, you are creating a situation where your child has to think. He will decide that having a friend is a good thing. She will want to share because sharing means having friends. This teaches a concern for others as opposed to the child acting solely from self-interest.

Children, like adults, often feel alienated as a result of their problems and confusions. How many times have you said, "No one understands me," only to discover that there are dozens of others who have experienced the same problems you have? The same is true, though to an even greater degree, for a child. One method of developing a caring sensitivity for others is to show that he or she is *not* alone. Whatever gives your child pleasure or pain also will give other children the same sensations.

"You mean you were once a little girl like me, Mommy?" "You once played with dolls?" "You had hair on your head when you were a little boy, Daddy?" You know the questions. We find them adorable or frustrating but they all reveal a child's limited understanding.

When a child is hurt by an unthinking act of another child, the child is extremely upset. Yet the same child can get into a fight and deliberately throw stones, mud, or snowballs with the intent of hurting another. The child has not learned that harmful deeds eventually return to hurt those who do them.

How can you instill this idea into your child? One way is by talking with your child as the problem arises. "Suzie loves her new dress, Janie. If you push her in the mud, the dress will be dirty and she'll be very upset. Do you remember when you got those pretty black shoes you love? How would you have felt if someone had gotten them all dirty and marked? It's the same with Suzie. She's hurt because you want to make her new dress dirty, just as you'd feel about your shoes."

Asking a child to put herself in another's place is extremely effective. Let your child think about her reaction to the kind of situation you feel is wrong. "How would you feel if . . ." is a most effective way to calmly handle the matter. In general this has to be suggested to the child.

Once children realize they are doing something to another child that they would not want done to themselves, they stop. Punishing a child is meaningless if you do not help your child understand *why* what he or she has done is cruel and/or thoughtless. Teach your child to think of him- or herself as belonging to a larger world, a world in which all other children and adults share the same feelings, hopes, and fears. This builds the ability to love and care for others.

You can combine a training session in altruism with the meditation techniques discussed in the previous chapter. For example, one parent with whom I worked has taught her daughter to relax for five minutes a day. The girl, June, had been hyperactive. Part of this was a poor diet, something we easily corrected through nutrition. The remainder of the hyperactivity was not a problem at all. June was a naturally superactive child with a healthy curiosity about the world around.

June was taught to be quiet through the fractional relaxation technique. This was hard for her, at first. She was constantly moving about in my office, defiant and nervous about her sessions. I challenged her to be still for one minute by the clock. I told her I "knew" she couldn't do it. She became irate at my challenge and forced herself to sit, unmoving, for an entire minute. Her face sweated and her cheeks reddened from the exertion. However, she did make it and we had something on which to build.

Gradually I taught June to meditate, at the same time educating her parents to ensure that the family could work together. When June was able to relax five minutes, we showed her how to use the time to think. This made her daily behavior calmer and her learning capacity much greater.

Each time June did something wrong against another child, such as pushing a child from a swing, she would mentally relive it during her meditation period. "Put yourself in the other child's place," her father told her. "How would you feel if a big girl came up while you were swinging, pushed you to the ground, and took your swing?"

June reflected on her action and how she would feel if the situation were reversed. Then she voluntarily chose to return to the other child and apologize. She understood that the action was wrong, and recognized that, like herself, the other child must have felt anger and resentment. She wanted to treat the other children in a more constructive manner in the future for her own happiness and peace of mind. The meditation matured her. Punishment was unnecessary; she had learned her lesson. By placing herself in the other child's position during meditation, she changed through the positive action of self-understanding.

A child is never too young to have a sense of others and their feelings. Studies have been done of infants less than a year old who show compassion. For example, one infant's mother began choking on a piece of food at the dinner table. The baby was able to hear and see the mother's distress. The baby's face showed great concern and fear, not smiling again until reassured that the mother was alright.

In another instance, an infant became aware that her father was tickling her mother. The action was playful but the mother began begging her husband to stop. The infant became frightened over the mother's distress and let out a cry usually heard only when something was greatly upsetting. The moment the parents stopped and showed their baby that everything was fine, the infant relaxed and smiled.

Slightly older children try to comfort a parent who is not feeling well. A two- or three-year-old, seeing a parent with a headache, might crawl on the parent's lap, kiss or touch the parent's head to give comfort. One fifteen-month-old baby, seeing that his mother was tired, tried to give her his own bottle. This should be encouraged.

Another way to increase the loving quality of your small child is through storytelling. All children love picture storybooks. They enjoy hearing the repetition of the same tale and they also like to embellish the story with discussion. It is through this discussion of favorite stories that you can increase the loving qualities of your child.

For example, take the story of Cinderella. Ask your child how Cinderella might feel when she is not allowed to go to the ball. Discuss how your child might help her. Talk about the ways her fairy godmother plans for the wonderful night at the ball. You might even go further and talk about the nice things Cinderella would do after she marries the prince so that her family has a better life.

The possibilities are endless. You might have your child pretend to bring peanuts to an elephant who is featured in one story or help save Bambi from the forest fire. By taking the story beyond the plot line, you can help your child create loving scenarios that they can apply to their real-life encounters.

Another way to teach concern for others to a misbehaving child is to withdraw affection and to show disapproval while isolating your child from the problem area. This means interrupting a fight, for example, and sending your child to the bedroom while stressing your displeasure and pointing out how unhappy your child would feel if the situation had been reversed. The message you are giving is that hurting someone is not only wrong, but will also result in the withdrawal of your affection. Your child's need for being loved and the resulting sense of self-worth will be great enough to make him want to restrain from acting out his destructive urge. He or she knows the price won't be worth the hostile act.

Television can be an aid or a detriment in teaching your child to be sensitive to others, depending on how you use it. Many of the programs available to children are violent, and children have difficulty understanding what is pretend, and what is real. Their impressionable minds can apply what they see to real life.

The experiences of three-year-old Jimmy typify how what seems like innocent children's fare can affect younger children. Jimmy delighted in Walt Disney cartoons. His parents never censored them because they, too, had delighted in such shows when they were growing up. One evening Jimmy's father noticed his son was terrified while watching a Goofy cartoon during which Goofy was struck on the head.

Cartoon characters are forever being struck on the head, squished, launched violently into space, smashed against the ground, and otherwise treated in a manner which would kill a real person. Goofy was no exception. Jimmy adored Goofy and had a toy Goofy doll his parents brought with them from a California vacation. When Goofy was struck on the head, Jimmy rushed to the screen, patting the image he had been watching, saying "Poor Goofy. Goofy hurt. Goofy hurt." He hugged the set and desperately tried to comfort the cartoon character.

This caring attitude was nurtured by Jimmy's parents who also realized that Jimmy's television viewing would have to be carefully controlled.

The entertainment of television dramas comes from the sensational escape they provide. The majority of viewers will never have to suffer being mugged, beaten, shot, stabbed, chased, raped, kidnapped, tortured, and otherwise being either terrified or miserable. If they did, they would not want to watch it recreated on the screen. It is because our lives are so often routine and safe that we can view this often seamy melodrama as a chance to relax with a mindless, physically passive activity.

The problem with most television programming comes to our children who have few contacts with the world at large. They are in school, at home, or playing with a neighbor for most of their early years. Their understanding of life on the streets and the ways in which men and women are expected to behave in conflicts can be molded by what they see on television.

The worst effect television programming can have on children is that after a period of viewing such programming, violence can be accepted as normal. Human suffering is viewed casually, passively, and without connection. We teach our children, through many television programs, that they need not get involved. They need not care about others or take the trouble to go to the aid of someone who is suffering. Their reaction is one of thinking that what they view somehow isn't quite real. This passivity makes them less reflexive, less sensitive, less giving and caring. Their natural altruism is blunted and dulled.

Positive television programming, showing altruistic acts, is occasionally available. It is better for children but still must be taken in extreme moderation. So long as your child is viewing such actions vicariously, rather than testing his or her own responses in real-life situations, exceptional qualities may not be developed.

Ideally, television should be banished during a child's formative years, but this is not realistic. There is much that is good for children on television and there is intensive peer pressure to watch some programs. Thus one solution is to limit what your child watches.

Get involved with television programming which will interest your children. Watch cartoon shows, "Sesame Street," movies, reruns of old shows, and anything else which your child might want to see. Don't go by your memories of shows which were on the air while you were young. Don't assume that because something did not hurt your development, it will not be bad for your child. There is a good chance that the programs you watched *did* cause difficulties for you which you have overcome as a mature adult. What you want to do is decrease or eliminate as many problem factors related to your children's growth as possible. The less their mental and emotional growth is starved this way, the faster they will develop the exceptional qualities you are trying to nurture.

Study the content of the television shows to see how it might be perceived by a child's mind. You might enjoy a Bugs Bunny program in which a cartoon character is crushed by a steamroller, but most small children will see this as being real. Laughter results from relief or because they are developing the mistaken notion that hitting or flattening someone is only temporary and it is not painful. This is a distorted sense of reality.

A few years ago, a woman who had raised her children without owning a television set wrote a cookbook which became a best-seller. She was asked to appear on some television talk shows and decided to take her small children (five to nine years of age) along with her. They had never been outside the tiny, isolated community where they lived and she felt that the tour would broaden their understanding of the world. The tour also introduced them to television which they delighted in watching in the motel rooms while their mother appeared on local talk shows and at autograph signing parties held by bookstores promoting her book.

One afternoon the woman stepped through the door of the motel room and was hit on the head by her youngest child. He hit her with such force that she was taken to the hospital with a possible concussion. She was fine but her child was confused. He was imitating something he had seen on a children's program and thought his mother would have stars appear over her head, walk around looking silly, then have everyone burst into laughter. He had no conception that what he was doing in real life would cause pain, suffering, and possibly, quite serious injury.

The child had been watching television and had no understanding that there was a difference between what was seen on television and what was real life. This is an extreme example of naiveté but does point out how the messages given by much of current television programming can distort reality in a child's mind. Constant exposure to violence gives children a false sense of reality, a lack of sensitivity toward others, and a tendency to observe problems vicariously. The child needs to identify with them through personal involvement in order to develop exceptional characteristics.

Have your children watch those shows which do not have violence, even if it means cutting back some of the shows you enjoy. This means eliminating most cartoon shows, police action shows, and melodramas. When quality programming has some violence to it, such as a documentary on Nazi Germany or a quality drama that takes place during the Civil War, discuss the show when it is over. Talk about why wars sometimes happen, why killing and hurting others is not acceptable. The violence should be understood as a flaw in human nature, something each individual must try to transcend. Compassion should be instilled toward the victims of such tragedies who are part of the drama of thousands of years of civilization.

Occasionally your children will watch the cartoon programs, reruns of the Three Stooges, and similarly violent programs supposedly meant for the young. It is extremely important to discuss the difference between fantasy and reality at such times. It is also essential that you go into the concept that there are repercussions from such violence. You must talk about the victim's pain and encourage compassion. Ideally you will help your child reach a point where he or she does not want to watch programs which have only violence because your child cares too much about the victim.

There is another problem with television which relates to the nutrition information in the earlier chapter. Daytime television watching keeps children indoors. Children, like adults, need exercise in the sunlight.

Some parents feel that teaching their children to be giving, loving individuals will make "sissies" of them. They worry that a child who is raised to see violence as wrong, to be concerned about the pain of others, will be the target for the neighborhood bully. However, the one does not lead to the other.

A child raised to care for others can still learn to stand even more forcefully for what is right, fair, and proper. A child who loves others does not let himself or herself be victimized by a schoolyard bully. The child who respects others insists upon personal respect. Caring and giving are the exceptional qualities of the best of humans; they are signs of strength.

Remember that your child is naturally giving and loving. We can nurture our children, working with them to understand and value loving others. Always remember that the ability to give selflessly is natural. The parent who wants an exceptional child merely supports what is inherent. By following the examples in this chapter, you will find that you can take new pride in your exceptional child as your child displays love and gentleness toward everyone.

7

Communicating with Your Child, or How to Rap with a Toddler to a Teen

It is not the quantity of time you spend with your child but the quality, something I have tried to stress throughout this book. The parent who is benignly neglectful by night and works by day also can be the parent who is in touch with the child's needs. The overly involved parent is not necessarily focused on the child's real needs just because they are on the premises twenty-four hours a day. There are no hard-and-fast rules.

There are two important aspects of communication with your child. One is the direct interaction of talking and listening. The other is the more important: Because of your own intuition, feelings, and love for your child, you are a unique educator. Because of biological and emotional bonds, which provide you with the common sense and intuition to provide the most fertile ground for your child's full flowering you can communicate indirectly in any number of ways. No amount of reading theory by educators and psychologists can substitute for the unconditional caring that is transmitted verbally and nonverbally by parents in touch with their spontaneous and impulsive feelings toward their young.

Communication means finding a common ground. It is the said and unsaid loving feelings and positive desire for your child that makes you an immediate and unlearned expert. From that springs a commonsense interpretation of what will produce the result you want. You must believe in your ability to show the way for your child, and in the child's ability to see the way you are trying to show. It is a learning process, each step of the way of which will involve trial and error. By honestly searching for the style of child raising that expresses your values and world view, you will be giving the greatest gift you can give: the model of a unique independent individual—yourself with your faults and your strengths.

Some working parents, especially if they have been at home during the first few months of their children's lives and now must enter the job market, have feelings of guilt. They see that their time will be limited, perhaps compared with the contacts they remember from their parents when growing up a generation ago. However, the anxiety is unfounded as numerous studies have now revealed.

For example, take what is known as the "latchkey" program being introduced in a number of elementary schools. The term latchkey comes from the problem of parents who cannot be home when their children return from school. Their children must let themselves inside the house and take care of their own needs for an hour or more before at least one parent can return. The schools offering latchkey training show children how to mend clothing, do the wash, make a simple dinner, and handle other tasks. The children develop the exceptional qualities of early self-reliance and personal independence without being denied the emotional support of a loving, nurturing parent. Instead of being harmed by the parents' not being home, the child participates in household tasks. Such a child is given an early chance to develop the competency and responsibility that will prepare him or her for becoming exceptional.

Some parents feel that they must be constantly involved with structuring their children's activities. But some parents have the contrasting attitude that the child should learn to explore the world around, get his or her glass of water, figure out a puzzle, and do other tasks independently. These parents do not deny their children's needs. What they do is set up a situation for their children to become problem solvers, explorers, and self-starters. They teach the creative side of independence which gets them to an exceptional stage of development seldom achieved by children whose parents solve all their problems for them.

A child must experience frustrations to learn to overcome them. When a parent does a task that is within the child's ability, the parent is actually spoiling him. Such spoiling, though done out of love, is an impediment to your child's development. It brings with it special frustrations and limitations because she does not have a chance to develop a full sense of self-accomplishment.

When your child learns a new task, he or she gains self-confidence, and feels strong, competent, and able to learn other tasks which might once have seemed overwhelming. The more you do that he or she could handle with a little effort, the less your child will accept challenges. Children do not learn through descriptions. They learn from mental and physical involvement.

If you decide to break the habit of doing more than is necessary for your child, you may find that for the first week or two, life is a little uncomfortable. Your child, who has been accustomed to getting milk on command, is now being told to get it himself. There may be tears, a tantrum, or some other expression of frustration calculated to make you feel such great pity that you go back to doing the task for your child. Yet not yielding teaches self-reliance which will bring far greater happiness.

In addition to encouraging your children to fend for themselves, it is important that you learn to "yell," particularly after more rational approaches have failed. (No, I don't really mean that you should try to verbally dominate their lives with high-decibel screeching. I don't want you to come across as the drill sergeant in the army barking orders at the troops.) You are like a god to your child. You are the source of all wisdom, love, and understanding. Your wrath is feared and your love is cherished. Yet a child who retains this superparent view is not going to be happy for very long. One day a parent is going to come across as being human and the child will not know how to handle such an ordinary experience.

By "yelling," I really mean showing one part of a full range of common emotions. Explain when you are tired or angry. Get mad when that is an appropriate feeling. Show when you are hurt. Make certain your child understands the context and that you do not blame your child for actions outside his or her control. But don't try to hide your emotions, because this will prove unhealthy for both of you.

For example, let's say you have told your child for what seems like the thousandth time to pick up toys and get ready for bed. Or let's say she has just ridden the tricycle, which you have long made clear is for outside use only, right through your living room, knocking over a lamp, scraping the wall, and crashing into a chest of drawers. Or say he is whining because you refuse to make the rain stop falling. It is not abusing your child to express your anger. "Mommy and Daddy are people, too" is what you are saying. "We get tired and angry. There are limits to our patience."

Remember that the alternative is resentment. Unexpressed anger is repressed. Then pressure builds up your resentment and this blocks normal parental love. Instead of helping to develop an exceptional child, your resentment leads to withdrawal or rebellion because you feared to show your child that parents are humans, too.

Being angry and yelling can be done with love. This sounds like a contradiction but it really isn't. There is no reason why, in the midst of an argument where your personal exhaustion is causing you to overreact, you can't stop, hug your child, then either apologize or express your love. If you are wrong, say so. If your child is wrong, make that clear as well.

When one of my children was small, he decided to get up at five in the morning, day in and day out. His attitude seemed to be that the sun was up, the birds were singing, and Daddy should join him at the start of his wonderful new day. The trouble was that Daddy is a therapist whose workday often extends until eight or nine o'clock at night. I wanted to relax after work, to read, and talk with friends. Then I would go to bed late enough that having to awaken at five was exhausting. There was no reason my son couldn't stay in bed, amusing himself, until a more comfortable hour for me.

Finally I had had it. I was tired, angry, and my son had been warned time and time again. "It's five in the morning! It's too early for me to get up. I'm tired, and I've told you that I don't like to get up at five in the morning!"

"I'm mad at you!" I said, angrily. "I'm mad because you keep waking me up. Now I want you to stop waking me up like this!"

My son was hurt, both because I was mad and because I was spoiling his pleasure. "I want to wake you up!" he yelled back, and then I was really mad.

"If you wake me up again, I'm going to wake you up! I'm going to come into your room at twelve at night and wake you up when you want to be sleeping. I'm going to do to you what you've been doing to me."

My son was shocked. He had never thought about the possibility of my waking him when he wanted to sleep. "Would you really do that?" he asked, nervously.

"Yes, I would. Then you'd know what it feels like. I don't like your waking me each morning."

"Daddy . . ." he said, hesitantly. Then he smiled, understanding for the first time because he had seen me angry and I had said things which made him finally comprehend the problem. I smiled back, then took him in my arms and hugged him. That was the last morning he awakened me like that. From then on, he played happily in his room, amusing himself with blocks and picture books until the rest of the house was awake.

This type of reaction is constructive yelling. You are not using your anger to overwhelm your child or to terrorize him into obedience. You are just showing the human side of being a parent and following immediately with a reassuring expression of love.

Children actually grow faster when you are a human and not "supermom" or "superdad." Their understanding of your needs and pressures will free them from the constraints of false concepts. This gives them compassion and understanding which eventually leads to exceptional qualities.

Play can become an important form of communication between you and your child. If you can enter into it, you will find a conduit to your child's inner life—to a world limited only by both your imaginations.

Play is about illusion. It creates order in an imperfect world. It adorns and amplifies life for the child, takes it from the everyday level and gives the child a chance to bring to the surface his inner life and test it on the outside world. Play with other children creates a sense of community as they share the magic of the play world, and it gives the child the chance to take chances and achieve something difficult in a "safe" situation. Play in your child's life, whether it is with games like visualizations in his own personal retreat or with friends, is the opportunity to externalize what he knows.

In the early years when a child picks up a piece of food, feeling it, slowly separating meat from bones or carefully taking the skin from an orange, separating the sections, removing the pits, and generally making a mess, the child is learning texture, smell, size, and other information. It may be a messy way to fill his stomach, but it is a positive learning experience. Have you ever watched the older child balancing on a narrow rail, jumping from stone to stone in a river, or noticed how rich and complex his games are with miniature figures and blocks, where microcosmic worlds are invented and shared between friends? All of these are tests. Some are of tension and uncertainty, to see how far they can go in the same sense that adults gamble and compete in athletics. Some are to create an enchanted captivating world of imagination.

When a child first starts school, his or her active imagination, so important in play, can cause some minor misunderstandings. Children often misperceive the meaning of the way the teacher responds to them in class. If your child is called upon with less frequency one day than he or she was another day, your child might think that the teacher doesn't like him as much as before. It is necessary to stay alert should such misperceptions arise. You can do this by talking with your child, helping him or her to understand that the teacher's affection remains constant from day to day. It is the classroom conditions which are variable and which may determine who gets more attention at any given time.

Your child might be a little sad one day and see you lost in thought for a moment at that time. Instead of recognizing that you are simply thinking about something, your child may feel, "Daddy is sad because I've done something wrong. I'm sad because Daddy thinks I'm bad and that's why he's sad around me." You might be feeling marvelous. But your child sees himself at the center of both your and the teacher's actions and responses.

You should never be upset with your child for having this false impression. The immature mind is not always capable of seeing more than a single point of view. Objectivity is usually not a trait of childhood until around the age of six or seven. Thus you must reassure your child of your loving support. When he understands that there is more than one way to view what is going on, and sees your support, he will be happier and better able to grow.

Another example of projection comes with children at play. Suppose your child wants to spend time with Johnny and she spots Suzy looking over at the two of them together. She will fear that Johnny will leave to play only with Suzy. Instead of being able to express this, she will project negative feelings onto her. "Suzy is lonely and jealous of me because I'm playing with Johnny. She doesn't like me because Johnny's with me and not her."

It may be that Suzy has no interest in either child. Your child's projected fears can then build a barrier. She can forget the original reason for concern and reach a point where she does not like Suzy. The fact that Suzy has done nothing does not change this, since the projected fears have become real.

You, the parent, will have to be alert to problems as a result of projection. They can be much simpler than they seem. If your child expresses dislike for another child, quietly discuss the reasons why. Have him give specifics for what bothers him concerning the other child. In the case of the Johnny and Suzy incident, the conversation might go something like:

"Suzy hates me because I play with Johnny."

"Why would she do that?"

"She wants to play with Johnny when I'm playing with him. But she can't because Johnny's my friend."

"Johnny can be your friend and Suzy's friend, too, can't he?"

"No, he's my friend."

"But you have other friends. You play with Johnny and Billy and

Tammie. You can play with Billy and still think that Johnny's your friend, even though you're not playing with Johnny right then."

"I guess."

"If you can be friends with so many children, then Johnny can be your friend and Suzy's friend, too, can't he?"

"She had no right to come over when I was playing with Johnny."

"Maybe she didn't know you wanted to play with Johnny and nobody else."

"She knew. She's always butting in. I hate her."

"Maybe you feel that way because you think Johnny will like her better than he likes you."

"He wouldn't do that."

"No, he wouldn't. Johnny likes you, but he might like Suzy, too. That's okay, though, because you like other children just as you like Johnny. I don't think Suzy wanted to take Johnny away from you.

"Maybe when you were playing with Johnny, you were afraid that Suzy would ruin your time together. Maybe you were a little scared that Johnny would go away from you and you'd be all alone right then."

"I don't know. Maybe . . ."

"But Johnny isn't going to do that. I think that the next time you're playing and you see Suzy, maybe you could ask her to play with you. That way you would have a new friend. I don't think Johnny would mind and I'll bet Suzy would like that, too. You know how lonely you would feel if you saw other children at play and they didn't invite you to join them. I'll bet you could make Suzy feel better and have even more fun if she joins you."

What you say and how you handle this depends upon the age of your child. However, these incidents are going to arise throughout the formative years and it is important for you to take the time to truly understand what is happening. Your child cannot develop exceptional qualities unless you remove the barriers to understanding. Projection of feelings by one child onto another is one such barrier. By taking the time to talk it through, understanding what might be happening, both you and your child gain greater insight and a growth of love.

Projection of negative and unwanted feelings can find outlet in various forms other than outbursts with friends. All kinds of art are an important outlet. Here these feelings are transformed into an external expression outside himself. With a little guidance, he can look at their meaning objectively and recognize his more violent feelings and begin to master them. For instance, Johnny draws a picture of his father in red with frowning eyes—clearly an evil and angry representation. You talk to Johnny about his feelings toward his father and why he feels that way.

When a child first tries for creative expression through artwork, many parents mistakenly slightly stifle that creativity by projecting an adult's idea of progress onto what the child must be doing. They make the assumption that the child is trying to duplicate something on paper, which, after all, is what an adult artist does.

A child has different intentions. Painting and drawing are explorations of discovery. A child begins to understand the use of paint, crayons, and paper by seeing how everything fits together. A child makes color, shapes, and scribbles as experiments complete in themselves. The child is learning about both tools and colors with no other end in mind.

After the period of exploration comes the beginnings of control. This is still a time of experimentation when your child is learning to refine the scribbles into harmonious shapes. Your child might make circles, squares, or other designs with an obvious purpose, though still not related to any object.

Next comes the development of form and organization. Basically this means drawings with a purpose. The design is planned. Real shapes are visible. You can see that your child had a purpose other than just exploratory learning with whatever technique was used.

Finally there is the last stage of development—representation. Now your child is trying to recreate something. At this stage there is no problem with discussing what the child was trying to draw. He has definite purpose, thought, control, and a desire to duplicate an aspect of the perceived world around. When you discuss the drawings at this stage, the questions will not upset her sense of self-worth in terms of creative development. As crude as they may seem, here projection becomes creativity; the perceptions are a tangible form of personal art.

Paintings should be discussed while your child is at the easel. If she is in kindergarten, for example, a question such as "Would you tell me what you are painting?" will be most appropriate while your child is in the creative process of just finishing with it. Her attention is focused on the work and this is the best time to communicate. A child's attention span is limited enough so that discussing this much later will reduce her interest and the chance of intense interaction.

The idea of communication with your child during this time of creative expression is to increase his awareness of personal creativity. For example, suppose you are talking with a very small child and you want to avoid the trap of trying to make something representational before he has reached that stage of development. Make your sentences descriptive, though in ways which stay close to what your child has done. You might say:

"I see you are starting with red." Or "I see you are making a line which goes across." "I like the way you are making your brush go round and round and in nice shapes." Or "You are making a very nice, large shape."

You can also use this kind of expression to broaden your child's understanding. For example, suppose your child says, "I made green."

You will respond, "Yes, you did, but what sort of green is it? Is it a dark green or a light green?"

He might also start the conversation with a question. "What color did I make?" he might ask.

"It is hard to say," you reply. "Sort of tannish. It is sort of like the color of sand at the beach. What do you think?"

"I think it's sort of like skin color," your child might reply.

Another approach comes when he says, "This is a fire."

You might respond with, "See how strong your brush strokes are. They are like the strong flames of a fire."

"I'm finished."

"Let me see. I like the way the yellow is peeking out behind the blue here. What other colors can you show me?"

The entire series of dialogues is meant to increase your child's consciousness of art, shapes, the world around, and similar matters. You make comments and ask questions which will constantly encourage.

Remember that each child is unique and each progresses at his or her own pace. If you have several children, they will all be different. You cannot apply a set of rules to each age, since children of the same age can have widely varying maturity, intellect, and abilities. What matters is that you remain open and sensitive so that you can create a secure, loving environment that is always supportive.

As the parent of a growing child, your efforts at communication must always take into account the great distinction between internal feelings and outward actions. It is perfectly reasonable for you to expect your child to learn to control his or her outward actions. Your expectations as to the degree of this control will have to vary with your child's age. Far more can be expected from an older child than a younger one, yet all should be expected to show this degree of "civilizing."

Thoughts and feelings are quite another matter. A child cannot control thoughts and feelings, with the possible exception of the focused thinking used during meditation and visualization. Thoughts and feelings come uninvited into the mind. The limits and rules you make must be realistic for the outward actions and your child's age.

The direct expression of feelings is quite different from the physical acting out of these emotions. Your child should not have the right to go around smashing furniture when angry. He or she must develop the physical control to prevent acting out these emotions. On the other hand, it is only right to let your child have the freedom to express anger. Your child might say something to the effect of: "I'm angry. I want to break the coffee table to show you how angry I am. I feel like I want to hurt something, I'm so mad."

Such expression of feeling allows you to talk with your child about the cause of the anger and better ways to deal with it. You should not say, "That's a terrible thing to say. You shouldn't be so angry. The furniture is expensive and we have worked very hard to be able to buy it. You have no right to talk about breaking it."

Your child *does* have the right to want to break the furniture. Your child *does* have the right to express anger and frustration. Your child does *not* have the right to act destructively. That is the external control you must demand. The talk concerning the feelings is merely the allowing of the internal emotions to be expressed. This is healthy and important to emotional well-being.

When a child expresses extreme emotions, you can best help him by repeating what has been said. This should be done in your own words, expressing the same feeling to ensure that your child sees you understand. For example, suppose she says, "I hate my baby brother because he broke my airplane."

Instead of saying, "I understand how you feel," you should say something to the effect: "When your baby brother broke your airplane, you must have felt so much anger that you hated him." This lets your child know that you truly understand the emotions he or she is experiencing without making a committal concerning the problem. You then have an opening to continue, guiding your child's thinking.

"You worked hard to build that model. You play with it all the time. It was a special plane and you would be angry with anyone who broke it."

"Yes, and he did, and I hate him."

"You were like your baby brother once. You were clumsy and you didn't know how to play with things without hurting them. Babies learn by playing with things but they can break things while they're learning. That can make you angry."

"Yes, he's so clumsy. He can't even walk right, always falling over and bumping into things. And he's always in my toys."

"You used to explore the things in my purse and you'd get into the cupboards. You're the oldest so there weren't any toys around that weren't yours, but I'm sure you would have broken things, too. That's a regular part of growing up."

"Well, he didn't have to break my airplane. If he's so clumsy, he can just leave it alone."

"You're right. There are some things your baby brother is too young to be around. That's why we try to keep so many of our possessions out of his reach. It's like your plane. Where did you leave it when he got it?"

"It was on the floor of the living room. I told him not to go near it but he's such a dumb baby."

"He's curious, just as you were. And he doesn't have the ability to understand as you do. You've seen that when you've played with him. That's why you should keep special toys out of reach. It's no fun to have to put things away all the time but that's what you have to do when a baby's growing up. Remember when I gave you those high shelves for things after the baby started crawling?"

"Yes."

"Perhaps if you used them for special toys like some of your other models, there won't be another problem. You have every reason to be angry, but your baby brother is just too young to understand. That's why we have to plan for him messing up a lot and then put things out of his reach so we don't have anything more broken."

"I guess maybe I should have put it away. I guess maybe I knew he didn't listen as I do."

"I think you're right. We can't bring back your airplane but we can make sure nothing bad happens again. We'll just have to plan ahead."

"You know, maybe I don't really hate my baby brother. I mean, he better stay away from my stuff, but I guess maybe I should have moved that airplane. He's kind of dumb about good toys."

Notice how the parent in this hypothetical example never said the obvious, that the older child was the one who made the mistake? Instead the parent discussed the situation so that her child came to the conclusion that she saw from the start. The hostility was expressed, then handled constructively. Everyone learned from the experience and the child did not have to become defensive in addition to being angry.

Every act that is reinforced with love and praise is an act which is going to be repeated. Giving attention to the positive and ignoring the negative as much as is realistic will encourage your child to repeat such good behavior. Your loving attention is the greatest reward a child can have. Your actions are a powerful influence in bringing your child to an exceptional maturity.

The one problem most adults have in understanding and communicating with their children is the fact that they are adults. You have learned literally millions of concepts. You know an infinite variety of facts.

A child is fresh and new. All the basics which are a part of your complex way of thinking have yet to be explored. Try to view the world through the eyes of your growing boy or girl. Take a box of crayons and some paper. Draw lines, shapes, and other scribbles, watching the way the colors appear, the variations which take place and the general feel of playing with color on paper. Never mind that you, as an adult, are supposed to draw "something." Recapture the wonder of exploration.

Perhaps you could take clay and run it through your fingers. Feel the texture. Smell the material and play with it. Make different shapes, not worrying about how it will end, just doing what gives you pleasure. Put on a record of music from another culture. Then dance to the unfamiliar sounds and rhythms, moving your body to the music.

The important point of all this is to try and recapture what it is like to be small, to be learning, and growing without earlier experience. You want to become a child, if only briefly, to have an understanding of wonder about all that is new. It becomes easier to see why your child does things differently from what you might expect.

A variation of techniques learned in the earlier chapters can help stimulate conversation which provides growth for your child. The idea is to combine her imagination with your careful questioning to lead both of you to a greater awareness. Here are some examples of how this works.

Gerald was brought in by his parents who had been coming to my office for some time. The entire family was normal, well adjusted, and basically quite happy. Gerald's parents had been seeing me not because of a specific problem but because they wanted to find greater purpose in life. They would get up in the morning, go to work, have dinner, watch television, and go to bed. I had helped them gain a better understanding of alternative ways to live—the development of the mind, body, and emotions. They felt that Gerald could benefit from the same concepts, concepts expressed in this book.

Gerald was nine years old, with brown hair that seemed always a little uncombed. He was short for his age, thin, muscular, and athletic. He was getting excellent grades in school and was the kind of child any parent would be proud to have. Thus coming to see a therapist didn't make a great deal of sense to him.

"How do you feel about coming to see me?" I asked Gerald.

"I feel silly," he replied, a little embarrassed.

"Why do you think coming to see me is silly?"

"There's nothing wrong with me. I'm fine," he replied, and he was correct.

"Yes, you are fine," I said. "Your parents have told me a lot about you. You're doing well in school, your grades are high, you're popular, and you're quite an athlete, I understand. But, Gerald, no matter how good you are now, wouldn't you like to do even better?"

"Sure I would. Is it possible?"

"Yes, it's possible. No matter how good someone is, it's always possible to feel and do even better. Look, why don't we try an exercise I like to use and I'll show you. First, close your eyes."

Once Gerald had closed his eyes and relaxed a moment, I said, "I want you to think of yourself. Think of how you look when you look in the mirror. Take a picture in your mind and look at it. We'll call this picture A."

"Okay, I can see myself."

"Now look at yourself closely. Think about what you are like. Is there any way you can be better than you are? Is there any way you'd really like to improve yourself?"

"Sure there is. I could have better concentration. All my teachers say that if I could concentrate more on what I do, I'd do even better."

"Okay, then this is what I want you to visualize in your mind. I want you to take a second picture, side by side with picture A. This second picture is also of you but this time it is of the Gerald you want to be. This is you with the better concentration you would like to have. Can you picture yourself having better concentration?"

"Yes, I see the second picture."

"Good, now I want you to move into picture B. You are going to take the Gerald of picture A and step right into picture B, becoming picture B."

"Gee, that's difficult."

"I know, but try to do it. See how far you can go."

"Now I got it. I got one foot in the new picture but . . . this is silly . . . I can't get my other foot in the picture. I mean, they're just pictures, but the one foot won't go in."

When you are working with your child, it is a statement like this one that Gerald made which is your clue to a problem. The moment your child has a difficulty with the visualization exercise, you know you have a point for discussion. Gerald is trying to imagine himself concentrating better. I didn't know why making that step was hard for him but I intended to find out. The same is true with your child. What Gerald said was a signal to be alert to a problem he had not previously revealed, a problem I would be able to talk through with him thanks to the visualization trigger.

"Your problem is called resistance, Gerald. Why do you feel your foot won't go in the picture? If you go in the picture, then you'll have better concentration. What do you think will happen if you have better concentration?"

"I don't know," he said, a little anxious. "I really feel that if I had concentration I would . . . I don't know . . . I want to have it, but I don't know why. . . .

"Maybe I do know why. I guess if I had concentration, I wouldn't be able to watch so much television. When I watch television, I always tell my parents it's because I can't concentrate. That's what it is. I feel that I can't concentrate and that's why I watch TV. But if I did have concentration . . . If I did have concentration. . . ."

"What would happen if you did have concentration?"

"Well, if I did have concentration, then I wouldn't get to watch so much TV. You know, I never thought of that."

"Now try and get yourself into the picture. You know why you had trouble, so see if your understanding makes it easier to get into the picture."

"Now it's easy. I can get into the picture real easy."

"Let all those pictures disappear from your mind and get another picture in their place. This is a picture of the new Gerald who is able to concentrate. I want you to see that picture of the new Gerald and bring it into you, making it a part of your body." I repeated the technique learned earlier about visualizing the image on all sides, then drawing them into the body.

Gerald opened his eyes and I asked him how he felt. "Much better," he replied. "I think I really can concentrate much better than I could before."

After several visits and following the above routine, Gerald discovered that his concentration had improved. He earned higher grades and he began reading books which interested him, not just books he had to read for school. His teacher was astonished because his reading capacity rapidly increased to a level more in line with a child a year or two older. The visualization technique alone had made Gerald an exceptional child in a way which would not have been possible without this magic. Instead, it was the communication with him during this exercise which helped him understand that something was deliberately, though unconsciously, holding him back.

Gerald wanted to watch television and felt a little guilty about doing it so much. He managed to convince himself that he had less of a capacity to concentrate on reading and schoolwork than he actually had. Then he would say there were limits to his ability to handle homework, extracurricular assignments, and casual reading. Once he believed that, he felt perfectly justified watching far more television than he would watch if he had what he felt might be better for him.

Gerald's parents have started using the same visualization technique to improve their own communication.

Remember that every child can be better than he or she is right now. We use a tiny fraction of our mind, ten percent of capacity according to the estimates of some researchers, and the more you teach your child, the more exceptional your child will become.

It may seem that Gerald was being deprived of pleasure—television—through this technique. In fact, Gerald rarely really enjoyed television. The passive entertainment of the programs gave him a topic of conversation with the other children. When he began to read, he discovered that the adventure stories found in the library, both the classics and modern works, were far more exciting for him. The visualization exercise had broken through the barrier he had created and, when he was able to concentrate more fully, he discovered that the active use of his mind was the most exciting way to spend an evening.

This same situation relates to your child. You are not saying that one activity is bad and another is good, even if, inwardly, that is exactly what you feel. Instead you are saying that one activity is fun, but a different one, an activity you know taps exceptional qualities, is even better. This fact makes becoming an exceptional individual a delight for parent and child alike.

There are many different ways to uncover the secret dreams and fantasies in your child's mind. These are the areas which, when revealed, can help you better direct your child toward exceptional qualities. Gerald was one case history using a visualization approach. A variation was the case of Susan.

I have two kinds of children coming to see me in my practice. Some have problems. Their parents bring them to me to help find the cause and a way to modify their children's behavior. Others feel that my techniques can help the children go from being typical to being exceptional. It was toward this end that Susan came to see me.

Susan was ten years old, happy, and earning good grades in school. I talked with Susan about her schoolwork and home life, then took a piece of paper and some crayons and gave them to her. "I want you to think about yourself. Make a picture of yourself in your mind, then I want you to draw that image," I told her. "I don't care what you draw," I explained. "You can make a picture of a girl like you or you can use a symbol, an abstract pattern or anything else you wish. What matters is that this image is you."

Susan drew a figure that had a lot of black in back and blue in front. Since she chose these two specific colors, I assumed that they had meaning. This is the same assumption you would make if your child was doing this exercise under your direction. "Tell me what the black means," I said. "Tell me what the blue means."

"The blue is when I'm feeling good and feeling happy. The black is when I'm not feeling so happy."

"Okay, now I want you to do something else. I want you to write or talk about the thoughts you have about this image of yourself. You have both black and blue down. How does this relate to what you feel in school, at home, and anywhere else? Tell me anything you think relates, no matter how small. I'm really interested in understanding."

"I guess I could say that I see myself as being happy sometimes. This is the blue. And I see myself being unhappy other times."

"Why are you unhappy the other times?"

"Well, isn't everybody?"

"Yes, but why you?"

"I don't know. I guess because sometimes I don't do as good as I want in school or maybe sometimes I get out of bed late and have to rush to school or whatever."

"Now let's suppose you could change your drawing. What would you do so that you could make your drawing all blue?"

"Gee, I don't know."

"Let's try to find out. Why don't you take a deep breath, then close your eyes, and let your body relax. Let your feelings become calm. If you're nervous, try to let your mind float quietly above those nervous feelings. You can remain alert to what we are doing while still being calm, quiet. Now I want you to remember that picture of yourself. Try to imagine it in your head. Remember that one side is all blue, to represent being happy, and the other side is black, meaning unhappy. Now what is it that you would like to be?"

"I would like to be blue all the time."

"And what does the blue symbolize to you? What do you think about when you talk about the blue?"

"I guess it's sort of a daydream of mine, an image of how I would like to be."

"What is that secret daydream model of yours?" This was a rather leading question. I have found that all children have a mental image of themselves which seems to fit one of several categories. Some children like to think of themselves as being better than they are. Their fantasy image gives them almost superhuman powers. They are perfect, at the very least, and often try to fit the fantasy of being like a comic book hero.

Another fantasy a child has involves seeing him- or herself as the child wants to appear to others. The child is reasonably objective about him- or herself but has a role in mind that is somehow "better."

A third fantasy is that other people have a definite idea of who the child is and they refuse to see the child any other way. Sometimes the child sees this situation as being a good one, because others make the child nearly perfect. Other times he or she feels unfairly maligned. Neither image is based on how others really think or feel, however.

A fourth fantasy involves the child having a glamorous secret daydream model that is impractical, exaggerated, and unobtainable. A ten-year-old is going to instantly be discovered by a movie producer and become the next big star. Or the child is going to be offered the job of circus ringmaster. There are numerous variations, none of which is based in reality.

The fifth fantasy commonly seen is the child who again projects the feelings of others. This fantasy has people always wanting to change the child to eliminate his or her identity in a destructive way. This situation usually does not really exist, even though the child handles relationships as though it does.

Because of these different fantasies, I was eager for Susan to tell me her secret daydream. Once I knew which type it might be, it would be easier to help her.

"I want to be happy all the time," said Susan.

This is a common desire for most children. They want to live in a world dominated by only one emotion—joy. "Is this possible?" I asked.

"No, it really isn't," she told me.

"But let's suppose you could be happy all the time. Why don't you get a mental picture of yourself as you would look if you were happy all the time."

Susan was silent a moment. She was obviously thinking about the image of herself as a totally happy person all the time. Then she said, "Maybe I wouldn't like that at all. It would be boring. I would never know anything else but being happy all the time, so maybe I wouldn't even know I was happy because I've never been sad.

"No, I don't really want to be happy all the time." Susan smiled and added, "I guess I just want to be me all the time."

"Being Susan is a good thing to be. But why don't you get a picture of yourself being just Susan all the time. Tell me what that means to you."

"Being me all the time, I guess means just being myself and loving Mommy and Daddy. And Mommy and Daddy are loving me and I'm doing the best that I can do in school. I'm not pushing myself to be happy when I'm really not wanting to be happy, because when I push myself to be happy when I really don't feel happy, then I don't get happy. I get sad because I'm not happy and I feel like I should be. I get all mixed up inside and I think it's better to be sad than to be sad and think I have to be happy."

"Okay, Susan, get a picture of yourself just being yourself. Think of loving your mother and father, and of them loving you."

Susan did this and we followed the suggestions mentioned earlier. She placed the image in front of her, drawing it into herself. She placed it behind, on top, and so forth. This is basically what is done during the visualization exercise of meditation. The more Susan did this, the happier she became. There was a smile on her face as she said, "I don't have to try to be happy all the time. I can just be myself and that's good. I can be more relaxed now. I don't have to be anything but me."

Susan was quieter than she had been when we first talked. It was obvious that feeling as though she had to meet the unrealistic expectation of being happy all the time had troubled her. It seemed a minor problem, but minor problems can be major stumbling blocks to growing children who want to tap their exceptional qualities.

I followed up on Susan's home life and school activities for several months, checking with her parents to see how she was doing. Remember that this was a girl who had always been an achiever. She was a child of whom any parent would be proud. However, the fantasy of being happy all the time had caused her to be unable to tap her exceptional qualities. She had been spending considerable time worrying about why she couldn't be happy all the time. She was frustrated by the fact that she depressed herself further when she wanted to be happy during periods of sadness.

The result of accepting herself made Susan stop being so self-centered. Instead of wasting time being concerned about her own emotions and perceptions of the world, she could concentrate on reading, physical activities, friends, and other interests. She learned to think more clearly, to be able to focus her attention on one subject for prolonged periods, and truly began achieving more of her potential. Her grades improved and she became what her teacher called an exceptional student, a compliment which thrilled her parents. And it all started with these techniques you can use with your own child.

Mark was a seven-year-old. He was a television addict living in a fantasy world of comic heroes in which he was Superman or Batman.

"What do you want to be when you grow up, Mark?" I asked.

"Superman," he said, proudly, and as we talked, I realized that he was quite serious. Telling Mark that this was impossible would be too hard for him to handle. In fact, a child who is forced to face the unrealistic nature of such a dream might take your reaction to an extreme. The child might decide that he is either Superman or a "nothing." If he decides that he is worthless, he may gradually give up on life, deciding at this early age that he is a failure.

A California school system tried to motivate children six and over by a system of harsh grading. A study was conducted in which first-grade students who did poorly received a failing grade. The idea behind this was that if you shock a child with an F when "it doesn't matter," the child will try to do better. The child is supposed to reason, "I got an F and that is terrible. If I don't apply myself and do better quickly, I might get an F when I'm in junior high or high school. Then it's going on my college record and I might have my whole future destroyed. I'd better get myself in gear and start working harder."

A child does not reason in such a sophisticated manner, as the study quickly revealed. The typical failing first grader actually was thinking something to the effect of: "The teacher gave me an F because I'm no good. She wouldn't have done that if I wasn't stupid. Since I'm stupid, there's no way I'm ever going to learn schoolwork. I might as well daydream and play during class because I'm not going to be able to learn anything anyway. The teacher said so. I'll just do whatever I want and leave school as soon as Mommy and Daddy will let me. They're going to hate me because I'm so dumb, but that's what I am and I can't ever be better."

The result, the study found, was that children who fail in first grade are likely to remain failures. They give up because they see themselves as failures at a tender age. The skills a child shows in first grade are misleading. A child *can't fail* because the child's abilities are untested and unnurtured. Some children are quicker to grasp some concepts than others. When a child does not do as well as expected, the *teacher* quite possibly should get the failing grade as perhaps it is the teacher who has not communicated.

The school system conducting this study recognized the failings of the teachers when a child did poorly. Grades were eliminated and test scores of the children were used to evaluate the effectiveness of the teachers. If a child did poorly on a test, the teacher had to devise new methods for communicating the subject. In almost every case, this approach resulted in all the children in a classroom doing well, not just a few. Not every child could be taught the exact same way, a fact requiring a little more personal attention than would otherwise have been the case, but the results were worthwhile.

I always remember this incident when I am working with a child who has a fantasy of being too perfect. Telling Mark he could not be Superman would likely make him feel he had to be the opposite. Thus it was important to change his thinking without shattering his perceptions of himself.

I had Mark close his eyes and get a mental picture of himself.

Then, when he had this image, I had him describe it. Naturally he told me that he was dressed in a Superman cape. "That is the image of how you would like to be, Mark. Now I want you to get a second image of what you are like today. You want to grow up to be Superman but right now you are Mark, which I think is a very fine person to be. I want you to get a picture of Mark just as you are right now."

As Mark did this, I said, "Mark, when you see yourself as Superman, what do you think about?" My question was meant to uncover the slight problems or thinking flaws all children have when they have an exaggerated sense of what they want to be.

"I'm not really Superman," Mark said, a little sheepishly. "But I want to be Superman. I guess it's because I love Superman and I love Batman and I love Spiderman. I want them to be me. But maybe that's thinking something that's better than I really am."

"Being Superman is better than you really are because Superman does things people really can't do. He is so good, no one can be like him. But you can be Mark and have that be good. Superman helps people and Mark can help people. Superman tries to work hard and you can work hard. Superman tries to live a life supporting law and order and Mark does that when he obeys his parents, his teachers, and others. But Mark can't fly like Superman because no real person can fly. If you try to really be like Superman and do everything he does, it won't be possible. But when you try to be yourself, that's really wonderful."

Maybe Mark could never be Superman but I have seen many adults who try to be. They are the perfectionists, the overachievers, the people who constantly strive to be better than they are, never accepting themselves and their successes. No matter how far they go, they will never be happy with themselves. Often these people are overwhelmed by stress, dying of heart attacks or suffering from stress-related illnesses.

I was trying to eliminate this future stress. Mark needed to learn to like himself for himself in order to be a relaxed, fully happy adult.

The problems of childhood often come from misperceptions by the child refusing to recognize his or her fullest capabilities. A child can tap into exceptional qualities and become a complete person as long as misinterpretations and misperceptions do not intrude to create barriers. Unfortunately children are exposed to so many conflicting views and ideas that such confusion can occur. The visualization exercise helps you identify, then eliminate them for your child.

Mark relaxed after our talk. He worked hard in school, but no longer felt he had to be better than he was. He became satisfied with doing the best he could each day, never putting himself down in favor of a fantasy superhero.

In the cases of both Mark and Susan, the children had unrealistic expectations which were affecting their conscious actions without their realization. The reverse can also occur when a child has a self-image that is far worse than reality. In both extremes, it is essential for the child to come to grips with the fact that the real person has value. Your child is not objective about his or her own worth, and anything you say that reinforces that sense of being "no good" will work against helping.

Notice how I always stress the value of the child when talking about the secret dream. For example, when I talked about Mark wanting to be Superman, I also talked about how good Mark was as himself. It was a remark made to seem casual but it was the planting of a seed of self-support within him. I wanted to gently change his thinking, letting him know that he could give up his dream for a more realistic one and still like his new approach to himself. The same is true when you talk with your child. No matter how secure your child may seem, the reality is that children are often ill at ease with changes.

Jimmy was another ten-year-old child who came to see me because his parents thought I could help him reach his exceptional qualities. He had no problems known to his parents, but I quickly discovered a reason for concern when we tried the visualization technique. Jimmy told me that he was basically stupid, never really succeeding at anything he tried. "I'll never be good at anything. No matter how low I set my goals, I never seem to achieve anything."

"Jimmy, your eyes are closed and you are looking at a picture of yourself as someone who never gets anywhere. Now I want you to take that picture and throw it away. Mentally, just shake it off. It doesn't exist anymore. All the picture is doing is limiting you. It is keeping you from achieving and I want you to just throw it away. Can you do that?"

"Sure," he said, shaking his head as though he were really getting rid of something inside his head.

"Now I want you to think of a picture of yourself having all the qualities you would like. This is a picture of you as an achiever, someone who can succeed. You are competent, able to succeed at whatever goal you set for yourself. Have you done this?"

"Yes, but . . ."

"This is the real Jimmy, the intelligent, handsome, perfect Jimmy. This is the you that really exists when you are not held down by the weight of that old picture of yourself."

Jimmy began to relax, his face radiating happiness. "I see it. Yes, I think I can see me that way."

"Now let's take this picture further. What good qualities do you want to add to this image of yourself?"

"I . . . I want people to like me. I want people to really like me."

Next I told Jimmy how to get a strong image of people liking him, and then to draw it into himself. This is the visualization technique discussed in the meditation chapter, and it helped reinforce his new thinking. I also told Jimmy's parents to help him do this every day until he found that he always liked himself, that he stopped having negative feelings.

Jimmy improved very slowly. First he began trying various tasks that he had once avoided, tasks other children his age could handle, but which he was certain he would "mess up." Each success seemed to bolster his new self-image. Gradually he became bolder in what he would tackle and even more successful at what he did. His grades improved, his reading and math abilities leaped beyond his age level, and he entered the advanced classes. He began having more friends and everyone remarked that he changed. "I don't think I've changed, Dr. Green," Jimmy told me several months later. "I think I've just learned who I am and that's a lot more fun than I once thought."

When twelve-year-old Betty tried the visualization technique, she told me that she saw her ideal little girl as being herself in a pretty party dress. She just had her hair washed and nicely styled, and she was smiling happily.

"This is the way you want to be?" I asked.

"I don't know. It's the way Mommy and Daddy want me to be, so I guess it's what I like, too."

Betty was obviously quite different from Susan and her dream model. Betty wanted to please her mother and father. Her image was of a person who would seemingly give her parents pleasure. What concerned me was that I did not know if this was the way she wanted to see herself.

"Now I want you to get rid of that picture. I want you to shake that little girl out of your head. I want you to take a look at you, the real Betty, the Betty that you know comes from within yourself."

Betty was uncomfortable at first. She seemed to have difficulty trying to decide what to do next. Finally, after perhaps five minutes, she developed an image she said was the way she really wanted to be. "And what is that?" I asked.

"Well, I'm relaxed and it doesn't matter whether my hair is washed or not. I don't even have my party dress on. I'm wearing dungarees, but it's not because I'm naughty. I'm comfortable. I like dungarees, and Mommy and Daddy are smiling at me because they understand I'm happier this way. I feel really good about myself and I feel really good about all the people around me. And all the people feel good about me."

I talked with Betty's parents about her, after Betty had learned to reinforce this good image of herself. They realized that what they wanted for her was not what she really wanted for herself. They could see where she had gotten into the habit of trying to please them so much that she ignored her real sense of self. They also managed to show her that all they had ever wanted was for her to be happy. They would not have had that perfect party girl image for her had they not mistakenly thought that was Betty's ideal for herself. Through this family understanding, an understanding you will reach doing these same exercises with your own child, Betty began to tap her inner self. She was happier, able to achieve more, and was well on her way to becoming fully exceptional.

The next case history was eleven-year-old Meriam. Meriam's goal was to be extremely successful in school. She was smart, well behaved, and at the top of her class.

"Is this how you want to be?" I asked. This is a question you should be asking your own child when working this way. The majority of time, this is the way your child will want to be. However, occasionally the child is parroting someone else and it is in response to such a question that your child will face the truth.

"No," said Meriam. "This is really how my parents, my teachers, and some of the kids at school think I am." In other words, this was the projection of those around her into Meriam's self-image.

"How else do they want you to be?"

"Smart, clever, smiling, happy . . ." Meriam was creating her ideal person based on the desires of others. She had never really come to grips with who she was or could be. She had the image that others wanted for her.

"Then this isn't the way you see yourself? This isn't the way you want to be? Is this right?"

"Yes. They see Meriam as being happy all the time," she began, talking of herself as though she were someone else. "They always see Meriam wearing a pretty dress and always being clean, they always see Meriam getting top marks . . ."

"If that's how they see Meriam, how do you see her? What do you want to be and do? What do you want to have?"

Meriam, her eyes closed, said, "I see sunlight going through my body. I can see myself and all this light. The light's going from the top of my body to my toes. The light's going in through my head and out through my toes. That's how I want to be. I want to be light."

"Could you explain that a little more, Meriam?"

"I just want to be myself. I just want to feel light and I don't want to get into all this heavy . . . heaviness of being what other people want me to be. I just want to be myself. I just want to be light."

"When you say you feel heavy, do you mean you feel that

everyone is trying to get you to do and be what they want? Do you feel that you're being pressured by your parents and teachers to act the way they think you should act instead of the way you want to act?"

"Yes. That's it. I feel so light when I'm just being me."

This was a problem that wasn't a problem. Meriam was not being pressured by others. She had simply failed to express her own feelings and had gone along with the ideas of others. Her parents wanted her to achieve personal fulfillment in whatever way was right for her. Certainly they had their own ideas of an ideal, just as you do. Yet, also like yourself, they wanted their daughter to be exceptional, but her exceptional abilities might not fit their preconceived ideas. Thus they were quite comfortable in letting her be herself once they realized she had been agreeing to some of their ideas just to please them.

I had Meriam picture herself the way she wanted to be, then draw that image into herself, the standard reinforcement technique we have discussed previously. I also explained to her parents what I had learned and how to use the visualization approach to allow for complete communication in the future.

Sam was a ten-year-old child whose personal image was rather unusual. "I feel like I can't stand still when I see myself, Dr. Green. It's like my picture is moving. It's being pushed or pulled but nobody's doing it. It's like a movie I saw on television where invisible things were making this guy move all over the place and he never knew what was pushing him around."

"You're being pushed from one place to another?"

"Yes."

"What's the other place like?"

"I guess it's not really a place. I keep seeing me having to be good in class and having to be good in sports. I also see my parents loving me when I'm doing these things, but I don't think I'm really happy this way."

"You mean you're seeing yourself as others want you to be?"

"I guess so. I love my parents and if they want me to be a certain way, I think I should be that way, but I don't like it. I want to fight that, and that's wrong, isn't it?"

"How do you want to be?" I asked.

"Just me," he replied. I then had him use the techniques of shaking off the image that made him feel he was being pushed and pulled in all directions. I told him to shake off all the weight and the values others had for him. Then I had him be still and try to experience exactly how he felt as Sam. He was to create the image of himself with which he was comfortable, unrelated to what anyone else made him feel he should be.

Sam took a few minutes to consider himself in the role with which he was comfortable. Then he opened his eyes, excited by the new insight into himself. "You know, Dr. Green, I think I figured out what was stopping me from really being myself. I always thought other people were trying to change me. I never thought about what I wanted to be so much as I fought their changes. I was so busy fighting someone else's idea of what I should be like, I guess I never got to know myself."

Sam, like most children, was basically good, kind, and eager to please. His image of himself was not a great deal different from what others wanted him to be. He enjoyed schoolwork, was intelligent, and easily earned high grades on his own. However, when others wanted him to get high grades, the grades became the goal and he mentally rebelled. When he felt he could just enjoy the courses he loved, not being concerned with grades, his grades actually went higher. He learned the material and retained it because of his love for it. He did not work for grades because the grades simply reflected the learning he had done for the thrill of getting new knowledge. He achieved his parents' dreams, but he did it in a way that made him comfortable instead of inwardly rebellious.

Sometimes the visualization method can lead to an emotional release that will surprise you. There can be times when a child has a problem he or she never faces. Emotions lie just beneath the surface and will eventually erupt disproportionately to the actual problem. By uncovering these problems in the early stages, the emotions can be countered and your child returned to a state of normal peace.

Cindy was such a child. A twelve-year-old, she could picture herself being happy in school, with friends, and at home. She could picture herself having a warm, loving relationship with her parents. Yet when I asked her to draw this image into herself, she was unable to do it. Once again I had a warning sign that Cindy was having a problem with which she had yet to come to grips.

"What is happening that stops the image of yourself from coming in and being a part of you?"

"I don't know. I guess I'm just pissed at it."

"You're angry at the image?" I asked, surprised by her response and the frustration shown by her language.

"No, I'm angry at my Mommy and Daddy."

"Why?"

"I'm just angry at them, that's all."

"Tell me about the angry, Cindy."

"Okay, I'm angry at them because they don't come home at night. Mommy doesn't come home until eight or nine o'clock and by that time I'm tired and want to go to sleep. I want to see her but I'm just too tired to stay awake very long. It's no fun being with her then because I'm so sleepy so I never really get to be with her.

"And Daddy's the same way. He doesn't get home until eight or nine o'clock either. They're always working. They think it's more important to work and make money than to spend time with me." Her voice was filled with anger and frustration. She continued talking, explaining her feelings, the intensity seeming to diminish the more she talked.

Finally Cindy became calm. She had expressed her rage and relaxed. Now she was able to handle the visualization and to make the image of loving her parents a part of her. Cindy's problem was a common one, overlooked because she had not expressed it. She had no understanding of her parents' jobs and the financial problems they faced. It was important for both of them to work, and their jobs prevented them from coming home until very late. They thought their daughter understood and, perhaps, superficially she did. However, deep inside she had come to the conclusion that her parents loved either their jobs or her, but not both.

Cindy's parents modified their way of living as best they could when they understood their daughter's concern. They could not change their time schedules of work and the family expenses were such that cutting back was not realistic. Instead, they started reassuring Cindy of their love. They called her during breaks on the job, talking with her about her schoolday and any problems she had. If anything was happening that was important for Cindy, they would discuss it the moment they came home, not even taking the time to personally unwind. Then, on weekends, the bulk of the day belonged to Cindy. They gave her intense time with each of them, one person being with Cindy while the other did chores, then reversing this approach. They also spent concentrated time as a family unit.

As the family relationship intensified happily, Cindy's parents also took time every week or two to communicate using visualization. This helped their daughter achieve goals for character development she set for herself and helped alert all of them to developing problems. By dealing with hurt feelings and confusion about personal matters when they were still minor, tension did not build to block the growth of exceptional qualities. Thus Cindy was able to improve in school and more completely enjoy the world around her.

It is important to note that the suppression of feelings happens for acceptable reasons. Cindy knew she was loved but needed extra reassurance during a problem time in her life. She felt guilty asking for more attention, yet her parents would have changed for her as much as possible the moment they were made aware of the problem. Once the family learned how to use the visualization technique as a trigger for greater communication, they became strongly emotionally bonded. Future problems were caught the moment they arose and did not reach the stage where they could hinder Cindy's achieving exceptional development.

Your child needs to become aware of his or her entire self. Sit together and have her get a mental picture of the way she wants to be. Then she draws that picture into herself, reinforcing all that is good and positive.

Keep in mind that your child's image will never be totally perfect. The image is going to be better than he has been. Your child is always reaching toward perfection and a better way to live. However, true perfection is not a realistic goal for any child. You are seeking positive growth and personal development greater than in the past. This means personal success, a thorough enjoyment of life, and a resulting high productivity. The result is an adult who will be respected, admired, and comfortable.

In conclusion, I want to remind you of the one other benefit of communication you should never overlook. This is the fact that you will come to truly know and more completely love your child. Your child is a delightful human being, a fact many parents fail to realize because they don't always know how to find out. The exercises discussed here will bring you and your children closer together, forming a bond of love and growth greater than any you might have thought possible.

8

Bedtime Manners to Sleep By

Sleep is a transition that children are ambivalent about. There are ways that a parent can make going to sleep desirable and enjoyable for them.

No matter what else you may do to help your child realize his or her inner exceptional qualities, it will be more difficult to achieve if you have not helped your child obtain adequate rest.

Sleep is not the simple process most of us once thought. There was a time when everyone assumed that you were either asleep and rested or awake and tired. However, people who slept poorly or used sleeping medication found that they were not rested. Complaints of this lack of rest despite being unconscious several hours each night led to more serious study and the eventual discovery that sleep comes in different layers.

Experiments into the different brain waves of sleep revealed several levels. The first level of sleep is so light, anyone awakening during this period would be certain he or she had never been unconscious. There is an assumption that the person is continuously aware of the surrounding activity, even though brain-wave studies indicate the person is asleep. However, during this period the mind frequently relives the day's activities, drifting through what has happened, though not really thinking about such things as a conscious person would. The thoughts are like passing clouds. You see, but never really become involved with them. Just saying your child's name is enough to get an instant response of "I wasn't asleep."

The second stage of sleep is deeper. The ability to see is lost. The mental images which flash through the mind are often unrelated fantasies. They may go back several months or touch upon anything in the unconscious memory. Most people spend at least twenty minutes at this second level, twice as long as in the first stage of sleep.

In the third level of sleep there are obvious brain-wave changes, a lowering of body temperature, and a drop in blood pressure. If your child is a restless sleeper, this is when he will begin moving about in bed. Your child may talk or mutter. Dreams are frequent but she is not likely to remember them unless awakened, an action which takes considerably more effort than during the first two stages.

The fourth stage of sleep is extremely deep. Your child is completely relaxed and has no conscious control of his or her body. Small babies may wet their beds during sleep because of the lack of controls at this stage. The same is true for older children whose bed-wetting is involuntary. Once again, this is a stage lasting about twenty minutes.

Children and adults usually take one and a half hours on the average to work through this cycle of sleep. Often it is repeated several times, your child drifting from the fourth stage back to the second, then back to the fourth and so forth. There is no sudden trip from first to fourth stages.

The fourth stage of sleep is also called the REM—rapid eye movement—level. The eyes move quickly when your child is relaxed in the deepest level of sleep. The body is completely relaxed, the mouth often resting open.

Children and adults need varying amounts of sleep. We talk about how it is essential for an adult to get eight hours of sleep a night. In reality, people's needs vary from as little as four or five hours to as many as nine hours. What matters is the amount of REM sleep, since this determines true rest.

Anyone who has taken a sleeping pill has noticed that after sleeping for eight hours, there often is no feeling of being fully rested. The reason is that you have not been allowed to obtain REM sleep. At this writing, there is no pharmaceutical on the market which can help you achieve REM sleep. The medication may break a pattern of wakefulness but that does not mean it supplies true rest. Fortunately there are nutritional substances which can help you achieve REM sleep. These vitamins and minerals are good for your children as well.

You, as a parent, may have some difficulty handling your child's natural sleeping pattern. Children simply do not do what adults want them to do. They do not have a consistent sleep pattern which fits with what we like to think is proper. Each age has different problems and reactions to sleep which most of us have now forgotten. It is only with older children and adults that sleep is fairly consistent in the way it is achieved.

Take a typical three-year-old, for example. Many three-year-olds seem to have an active nightlife. For example, we would put our three-year-old to bed, telling him we loved him and would see him in the morning. He would smile, shut his eyes, and go instantly to sleep, the perfect picture of an angel.

Some time in the middle of the night, the angel turned into a curious devil. He would climb from his bed and begin his nocturnal wanderings. There would be a trip to the bathroom, play with his cars, and then the investigation of our room to see if we were asleep. After anywhere from a few minutes to over an hour, our son would suddenly decide that it was the middle of the night, he really was tired, and perhaps it was time to get more sleep. He would drop in his tracks, sleeping wherever he would happen to be. We have found him on the couch, curled up on a chair, in the middle of the living room, on the floor of the kitchen, and in various other locations.

The wanderings were worrisome. I knew they were normal but I kept worrying about his playing with matches, turning on the gas stove, or even unlocking the door and wandering down to the elevator in the hall. Eventually he got over this habit and spent the night in bed, letting my wife and me breathe easier.

Before we explore normal sleep patterns and occasional problems your child may encounter, I want to stress the need to provide bedtime security for your child from the moment he or she is born.

Earlier in this book I mentioned how peek-a-boo teaches a child that a loved one returns. Some of this learning seems to disappear when your baby or small child awakens in the middle of the night in bed with no one around. "Where is everybody? Why am I alone? Will anyone ever return?" are the questions racing unanswered through the child's mind. The only response many children make is the wail of terror which brings you running from your bedroom.

The answer to this problem is always to reassure your baby at bedtime. "Good night. I love you. I will be here in the morning. I love you. See you in the morning." Such a statement, or your own variation, will eventually be understood by your child.

Good sleeping habits begin in infancy. What is the answer to the crying and fussing of the infant whose sleeping habits you are trying to regulate as much as possible? One is to make holding and rocking your baby part of the bedtime ritual. The rocking provides a sense of harmony for your child's equilibrium. This creates drowsiness which quickly puts your baby to sleep.

Between eight and twelve weeks, the isolation of sleep can create a situation where the baby rebels. A baby who cries for no apparent reason usually does have a problem, but it is different from a cry caused by hunger or pain, such as from a pin that has pricked the skin. Give your baby a light to look at, perhaps taking the baby from the darkened crib into the lighted kitchen or living room. Many babies hunger not only for food but also light and activity. When they again see people and brightness, they relax and go back to sleep.

Music can be helpful. A radio playing softly, or a stereo can prove soothing. No matter what your musical taste, experiment with the music. Some babies relax with any music.

Once a child has seen that which is important to him—light, people, or whatever, a gentle rocking and loving touch will help your baby sleep comfortably. Even at an early age, talk with your child about having a room of his own, being in the dark, and going to sleep despite the fact that others, perhaps even older brothers and sisters, are still awake. At first there is no comprehension, though the soft, soothing words of you and your spouse act like a sleeping medication.

Then, when there is understanding, the words themselves create the sense of calm.

What happens when he cries after being laid to rest and you know your baby is neither hungry nor in need of a diaper change? Many pediatricians say to just let your baby cry himself to sleep. The baby only wants attention and will try to manipulate you if you allow this to occur.

My feeling is that the idea of ignoring your baby is nonsense. Most loving parents have to check on the cries of their children just in case something more is wrong than orneriness at bedtime. Those who manage to steel themselves enough to let the baby cry may have a baby whose whimpers turn to screams of terror. This can be psychologically damaging for a baby. Thus I think you should respond.

When your baby cries at bedtime because something is wrong and the methods mentioned haven't worked, gently rock him, talk to him. Hold your baby in the crib, softly stroking the forehead and back. Touch and talk quietly, reassuring your baby that she is loved and safe. This makes it very clear that it is bedtime and you are not there to play games. You are *there*, though, and it is safe and sleep is all right.

The problems come when parents turn this period into what the baby sees as a game. Some parents bring extra bottles or go bouncing around the floor, playing with the baby to wear him out. They forget that the baby was already tired and is just feeling a little insecure. Reassurance brings sleep. The games result in your baby's seeing that crying is a way to get a new playtime. By avoiding the games, you are satisfying a real need of your baby's without creating problems for yourself.

By the time a child is a year old, he or she will develop methods for going to sleep. These include self-rocking, sucking a thumb, and other techniques which may continue through the preschool years.

Two-year-olds are constantly testing their parents at bedtime. "If I do not have one more story read to me, I will be unable to sleep for the next forty years, my hair will fall out, and I will develop an incurable skin rash." "I need another glass of water or, instead of sleeping, my tongue will turn into sand, and fall from my mouth." "I must go to the bathroom one more time or I will never last the night, even though this is my tenth trip in the last five minutes." The "I must have one more's" are typical of this age and rather frustrating for the parents. This is the game of the two-year-old at bedtime, and you must separate the genuine needs from the foolish wants.

The "just one more" syndrome is really your child wanting additional attention. Your child doesn't want water or a story, your child wants you. This is often a time of both insecurity and orneriness testing, the two so intermingled that it is sometimes hard to tell which is which.

Try to teach your child that if attention is desired, attention should be requested. "Do you really want to hear another story, or do you just want Mommy and Daddy to give you some attention before you go to sleep?" you might ask. Try to get your child to tell you what is really desired. When you do this, your child will be quite honest during the growing years ahead. You must respond to this need, of course, providing the attention for a few moments, even if you have something else you want to do. It is better to miss a few minutes of television, read a little less in your book, or get a slightly later start on your evening out than to deny your child your presence when it is desired. This is quite different from the game of testing, as you will quickly see the moment your child begins asking for attention when that is what is wanted.

A loving firmness is needed for the testing which goes on at age two. Certain rituals are common. Your child might really need a drink, want to hear a certain story, need a favorite toy, and perhaps make one or two other demands every night. Follow this ritual, then give your child a kiss, stress that you love him, that you will see him in the morning, and that you are tired, too. Then leave the room, slowly and quietly. Your child might cry out once or twice, but usually he will go right to sleep.

Sometimes your child will have additional demands. These may be real or they may be games. When this occurs, come back into the bedroom, firmly taking charge. "I love you very much. It is now bedtime and you must go to sleep. I'm not coming back again tonight because this is sleep time. I will see you in the morning. I love you and it's time to sleep."

On rare occasions it seems as though nothing works. Your two-year-old simply will not settle down. Your firmness holds no terror. Punishment seems inappropriate, yet you don't quite know what to do. At such times, ask your child why he or she can't fall asleep. Find out what is wrong. Make your child verbalize the cause of whatever actions are frustrating you and keeping you from relaxing. There genuinely may be a concern, a fear, or some problem. Usually there isn't and your child is unable to give a reason. At that moment, he realizes, just as you do, that he is really being naughty. You explain that since there is no reason, you are not coming back that night. You love him but it is bedtime and he must be quiet.

Upon leaving the room, there may be a certain amount of crying out. By this time your child is probably exhausted, cranky, thoroughly "rotten," and just carries on. Now is the time to leave him alone. You have responded several times, there have been no real problems except that your child does not want to go to sleep, so stay out. However, do stay alert to the type of cry. If it switches from one of anger and frustration to one you know is a cry of pain or need, then go back in. Otherwise your child will cry himself to sleep.

By around age two and a half, there is a ritual to bedtime. There must be certain toys, perhaps a certain pillow. A kiss must be placed in the same spot. Stories may be identical for weeks at a time, the order of the stories being constant. It is all rather boring for the parent but essential for your child. Fortunately you can easily learn the ritual, follow it, and have no further problems. This is all quite natural and gets her to sleep more quickly than trying to fight it.

The three-year-old usually goes to sleep willingly and falls asleep easily. Nocturnal wanderings are fairly common and not cause for alarm. Certain precautions should be taken, though, for your child's protection. For example, any open steps should be guarded by a child-proof gate sold for this purpose in many hardware stores. This will keep her from tumbling down the steps in the dark.

Many three- and four-year-olds favor one parent at bedtime, often the mother. Having five or ten minutes alone with this parent just before going to sleep also helps relax her.

The nocturnal wanderings occasionally lead your child into your bedroom. He will want to climb into bed with you, a potential habit it is best to discourage from the start. Explain that when he comes into your bed, none of you will be rested enough in the morning to enjoy whatever his favorite activity might be.

Take your child back to bed, either carrying him or walking with him. Lay him down, talk with him, then gently but firmly say goodnight. The following night, stress to your child that you know he or she will stay in bed. This is said just before sleep and gradually reinforces the concept that such night travels are not going to be tolerated. Your child is loved, but that loving does not mean that he or she can sleep in your bed. No matter what the sleep problem, your child should always be comforted in his or her own bed.

Parents of a newborn often live in a one-bedroom apartment which requires them to keep the crib in their bedroom. However, even in such a situation a distinct separation must be made. When it is bedtime for you and your spouse, wheel the crib into the living room so that you have privacy and your baby knows that now is the time for sleeping. It is never wise to have a baby raised in your bedroom even if this is the most convenient place to keep the crib during the waking hours.

The majority of experts in the field of child psychology warn against letting even infants see the parents making love. Seeing sexual relations is quite different from letting the baby see examples of tenderness, loving, touching, and other aspects of deep affection shared throughout the day. Sexual relations are so radically different in appearance that all children have trouble understanding what is happening. They can create fantasies which will cause them problems in later years. No one is certain how young an infant has to be before the sight of sexual relations registers in the mind, though it is at least by three months. Thus it is essential that you keep the baby in a different room during this period. Wheeling the baby into the living room accomplishes this end and results in your child having a distinct sense of the separation between sleeping and waking.

By five years of age children may have frequent nightmares. These are quite normal and reassurance should be given in your child's bedroom. Often the dreams are of wild creatures and your child is afraid to go back to sleep. Repeated assurances may be necessary. Fortunately these night terrors do not continue for very long, though they do cause a certain amount of sleeplessness for you during the period when they are frequent.

Small children have all manner of fears at bedtime. A four-year-old may need a small night-light in the room. Some four-year-olds want flashlights to keep under their pillows, though they will usually wear out the batteries so fast that a night-light plugged into the wall is preferable.

The dangers of moving shadows, burglars under the bed, and wild animals lurking in a closet are quite real to your child. They should not be ridiculed. If anything, wild animals should be shooed from the room, the underside of the bed checked for burglars, and your child's bed angled so that passing cars and other light sources do not create shadows in his line of sight.

The patterns of sleep and the need for sleep vary with age. An infant usually has about as much sleep as an adult has time being awake. Within four months, most infants need just under fifteen hours of sleep each day. The exact amount will be unique to your child and is best determined by awakening your child at the same time each day. You will quickly see when he or she is tired and needs either a nap or prolonged rest. This also helps you establish a schedule which is best for everyone rather than being forced to accommodate yourself to the self-regulation of an infant.

As children get older, sleep patterns can be a problem. Larry was brought to see me because he was not getting enough sleep. He claimed that he didn't need it, yet he was having trouble in school. He was an irritable, frequently yawning, obviously tired seven-year-old who simply did not want to sleep.

Medical tests had been run on Larry and he was in perfect health. The doctor had suggested medication but his parents felt that was foolish. A child has no business taking sleeping medication when such pharmaceuticals are potentially dangerous even for adults.

My answer, after checking Larry's diet to be certain he wasn't being stimulated by sugar and other processed foods known to cause hyperactivity, was to prescribe nature's sleeping medication. This is warm milk, which releases the natural amino acid tryptophane into the system, which brings about sleep. I also suggested that the warm milk have a few drops of vanilla and some nutmeg added to enhance the flavor if Larry did not like the taste of plain milk.

I told Larry's parents that the warm milk could be supplemented at first by a natural calcium-magnesium combination called dolomite. Some manufacturers boost the price by combining it with iron, vitamin C, or some other vitamin. Buy the natural dolomite which is a standard combination of 323 mg. magnesium and 609 mg. calcium and give the child of this age two tablets at bedtime with the warm milk. Older children can be brought to the adult level which is four tablets at a time.

Dolomite is a natural mineral that cannot be taken in overdose or cause side effects, because it is not a chemical or foreign substance to the body, as all sleeping medications are. It does not interfere with your sleep pattern. Sleep comes naturally and reaches the REM level with ease.

Larry did not sleep perfectly the first night. It took two or three days of dolomite, warm milk, and quiet, loving attention from his parents. They did not overreact to his problem; they accepted it and encouraged him to rest.

Within a week Larry was a changed child. He was sleeping well and using the other techniques of this book—because he was alert enough to use them. He gradually substituted the meditation technique for the warm milk and dolomite. His grades began to rise in school and he showed his teacher and parents his exceptional qualities which had been masked by the sleep difficulty.

Sometimes sleep problems are easily handled. Five-year-old Jenny's parents were concerned because she never napped. They would argue when they found her quietly playing in her room during naptime. This created stress which led to difficulty sleeping at night. Once her parents realized that, unlike other children her age, Jenny simply did not need that much sleep, everything was fine. The pressure was off and Jenny flourished with only her nighttime sleep.

Four-year-old Billy's parents were upset because he always awakened earlier than they wanted to rise. Again the answer was simple. They kept him up an hour later at night.

Sometimes sleep problems reflect difficulty in another area of a child's life. Seven-year-old Sylvia came to see me because her mother was concerned with her wetting the bed. "Why do you wet your bed?" I asked.

"It's awful. I hate going to bed at night. I'm afraid to go to bed because I know that as soon as I go to bed, I'm going to wet it and I know that as soon as I wet the bed, then Mommy's going to get mad at me. The doctor said I'm okay so Mommy yells at me when I wet it. But I wet anyway and then I'm scared. Usually I'm scared to go to sleep because I know that I'm going to wet the bed and Mommy will yell and . . ." She began crying.

"When did you start wetting the bed?"

"I don't know. When Daddy went away. I guess. I think that was six months ago."

It was obvious that if there was nothing physically wrong with Sylvia and if the bed-wetting started only after her father went away. I felt that only by understanding Sylvia's reasoning about all this could I help her. "Why did Daddy go away?"

"Mommy made him go away."

"Is he coming back?"

"I don't think he's ever coming back. Mommy made him go away and I don't think Mommy's letting him come back."

"What were Mommy and Daddy like when they were together with you?"

"They were always fighting. I used to hear them fighting when I was in bed. They did it at night. Sometimes they'd fight all weekend and make me stay outside so I wouldn't hear them, but I did. They'd fight all the time and then Mommy sent Daddy away."

The facts differed from Sylvia's perceptions. Her parents had been divorced six months earlier which her mother had never explained. Her father was having an affair and his wife found out about it. The couple divorced because he refused to give up his mistress whom he later married and took to Colorado. Sylvia's mother thought she was protecting the child by not telling the truth. Instead, the avoidance of the truth led to the nighttime problems; Sylvia unconsciously used the bed-wetting to fight her mother whom she blamed for causing her father to disappear.

Sylvia was rebelling in other ways, too. She was a gifted pianist whose work seemed to foreshadow a professional career. She loved the piano and it thrilled her mother to hear her play. However, during this period she gradually played less and less until she stopped entirely. Her mother was so concerned with the nighttime incidents that she did not relate the piano situation to the other.

I talked with Sylvia's mother about what had happened. We agreed that it was best to tell Sylvia the truth because the truth, no matter how upsetting, is always easier to handle than what is built up in the imagination.

"Your father and I married because we loved each other very much. We decided to have a child because we loved each other and you were the result. Your father still loves you and I love you because parents always love their children. But parents don't always love each other. Now your father loves somebody else and we have decided to get a divorce. A divorce means that he is going to live with somebody else and I am going to live with you and take care of you. He is living in Colorado with another woman."

As soon as Sylvia learned the truth, she stopped wetting her bed and returned to the piano. It was easy to handle her emotional problems toward the divorce once she faced them. It was Sylvia's fantasies about that problem that presented the block to their solution and to her growth. Now that was over and Sylvia was able to enter a special school for gifted child musicians where she thrived.

The exceptional child is often an extremely sensitive child. This can lead to sleep problems which become the focus of concern for the parent. For example, nine-year-old Ricky was brought to me because he had hypersomnia, a condition in which a person sleeps far more than normal. The doctors he had seen had talked of schizophrenia and other severe mental disturbances as being the possible cause. They had placed him on pharmaceuticals, the side effects of which were keeping him from being able to function at full capacity. He had shown exceptional qualities until a year earlier and now was sleeping much of the time, doing poorly in school, and generally having a difficult time.

I decided to work with Ricky's parents to improve their ability to communicate with each other. We worked on the visualization and meditation techniques, along with the general methods for communication. His parents told me that the problem had begun a year earlier so I had them ask Ricky what happened at that time which caused him to need so much sleep.

"It's that baby," he said, angrily. "Mommy had that baby and now she doesn't love me anymore."

Sibling rivalry. It is as old as the biblical story of Cain and Abel, though it usually does not occur when children are five or more years older than their new baby brother or sister. After five years, the child has a well-ordered life, friends, and enough activities to ensure that the older child seldom resents the younger one.

Ricky was almost eight years old when the new baby arrived. His parents assumed that he was so involved with his own life that he would not be bothered by the attention a new baby must have during those helpless first few months. They didn't realize that his sleeping so much indicated that he needed to talk and they had not learned the communication methods which ensure exceptional children.

"They were only interested in that baby. I used to love to play the recorder. I decided to stop playing to see if they'd notice and they didn't. Nobody said anything about it. They didn't care. They didn't care about my recorder or me or anything. I figured, why should I try? Nobody loves me so I might just as well sleep as do anything. Nobody cares."

The moment the anger was out, Ricky's parents were able to talk and express their love for him. They explained that the baby had the demanding needs common to all newborns. The attention the baby received from necessity in no way displaced the love they felt for Ricky. With just this simple reassurance, everything changed. That first night, Ricky slept normally, awakening refreshed, and he was fine. He returned to an active childhood, taking up the recorder once again, and having a renewed interest in his schoolwork. He just needed the slight reassurance he received.

Insomnia is often caused by very simple matters which, with logical reasoning, you can handle easily. For example, your child has a late snack or a heavy meal around 7:30 or 8:00 P.M. This is quite common when both parents work. Rearranging the kind of meals, so that the last meal is a light one, is a simple way to avoid this problem.

Does your child watch television before going to bed and then have insomnia? Television may be a passive medium in the way it is viewed but your child can become extremely agitated from what is being watched. The elimination of television viewing late at night or a careful monitoring of what is being watched so that a change in shows reduces the agitation level can stop the problem. Remember that your child's perception of television seldom matches the reality of what is on the screen.

Babies also have separation anxiety as discussed earlier. When your baby has prolonged difficulty sleeping at night, often it is just a matter of being a little more sensitive than others to being away from you. The solution is to pay a little more attention to your baby at departure time until your baby truly comprehends that you will always return when the baby awakens.

Sleep is important for the development of exceptional qualities. By following the suggestions in this chapter, using the communication methods for uncovering hidden anxieties, and using dolomite and warm milk when necessary, your child should easily develop a normal, healthy pattern for regular sleep.

9

Coping with Problems

No matter how well developed your child's mind is, part of his growth pattern is to be subject to moodiness, depression, sibling rivalry—difficult parts of raising a child.

You may feel that if you follow the plan in this book, you have done everything you can for your child. Should problems arise after you have begun developing your child's exceptional qualities, you may fear you will have to turn to a full-time "expert" for help. Some of the work I do is with parents with just such concerns, and this is one of the reasons for this book. Your love and openness with your child are the greatest contributions anyone can make to your child during troubled times. There can be no professional therapeutic "fix" so effective as the support and confidence of a parent for his or her child.

Your child may have some problems which seem to indicate the need for outside help, but there may be several answers, at least some of which you will be able to handle without assistance. For example, such an extreme problem as childhood schizophrenia, an ailment that has caused some children to be institutionalized, now appears to have one dramatic source: an extreme reaction to sugar, food additives, and food dyes. Eliminating sugar and chemicals from the schizophrenic child's diet eliminates the symptoms in an estimated one-third of all such cases as well.

What is important to understand is that there is very little which affects your child which cannot be changed for the better. Do not be fooled by the labels placed on your child by outsiders. You know and love your child better than anyone, and are in a better position to help your child.

Take the case of Derek whose mother brought him to see me. Derek was a typical six-year-old, into everything and running all over the house until he dropped. He could easily wear out his mother, and she assumed this was normal. She had been practicing the concepts in this book and her son was already revealing a special interest and early skills in both music and art. Everything seemed perfect until Derek's grandmother pronounced him hyperactive after caring for the boy for an entire week.

"I've never seen anything like him," said the grandmother. "I had four children of my own and they were active children. I treated Derek just as I treated my own but he drove me crazy. I've never seen a child with so much energy. I couldn't keep up with him and I had no problem keeping up with my own. My next door neighbor's son is in medicine and he said that, from my description, Derek's obviously hyperactive. I'm telling you that if you don't try to get him on something to calm him down, you're going to have a real problem. My friend's son said that Ritalin used to be used and I think you better get some for him."

Derek's mother was horrified. She didn't believe in using pharmaceuticals to control behavior because she knew the side effects of such chemicals. She had also never considered her son to be different in any way. However, she respected her mother-in-law who had had the experience of raising four children.

"How old is your mother-in-law?" I asked.

"She's fifty-six. My husband was around thirty when we had Derek."

"And when did she have her children?"

"Right away. My husband's the youngest and I guess his mother was twenty-one or twenty-two when she had him."

"Then she was little more than a teenager when she was giving birth?"

"Yes, but what does that have to do with . . ."

"And now she's in her fifties. Is she an active woman?"

"Not really. She loves sitting around reading or watching television. She and her husband are avid bridge players and go out several nights a week to play. But I guess that's mental activity. Why?"

"Because she's remembering child raising at a time when she was young and filled with energy, just as you are. Now, being considerably older and sedentary, she's trying to relate to the same situation. That doesn't work. She's tired now, not because Derek has something wrong but simply because she isn't the same physically active person she was. She's assuming that Derek should be as easy to handle as her own children were and she's not facing the fact that he probably is that easy to control. She's the one who's changed, yet you're worried about her misperception."

"I never thought of that, Dr. Green. And you're right. My husband and I are very active people and Derek can be tiring even at that. Give me another thirty years of not doing much and I'd find him overwhelming."

Everyone tends to see someone else as an authority figure. It might be a schoolteacher, a psychologist, a pediatrician, or a mother-in-law who raised a large number of children. We want to have them give us the answers to our problems. We think that someone else can magically raise our children, while we are incapable of doing this perfectly natural act. The truth is that there is no problem you, as a parent, cannot handle. You can have an exceptional child and, when some difficulty arises, you can find the solution.

Always trust your "gut reaction" concerning your child and do not let yourself be influenced by someone else's label. The term "learning disability" may simply mean that your child is bored and that the teacher is not able to provide needed stimulation. It is always easier to blame the child than to see if the methods for teaching are as effective as they should be.

Hyperactivity often means only that the child can keep going longer than the adult. This is a little like the definition of nymphomania—any woman who wants sex more frequently than her lover. It is always easier to attack with a label than to try to understand the real problem. Unfortunately, if you are not aware of this possible game, it is easy to let "experts" influence what you do with your child. Many a child is temporarily institutionalized because the parents believed a label that should not have been used in the first place.

Many children suffer from stress-related problems. Janine was an eight-year-old girl who suffered from asthma. Since asthma is stress related, I felt that reducing Janine's stress could relieve or end the problem. This was counter to what her allergist and pediatrician believed. They agreed to let me try since my efforts would be neither dangerous nor in any way interfere with their medical treatment.

I gave Janine a lot of vitamin C—1000 mg. daily which is a fairly large amount for a child her age. Vitamin C handles internal stress and is nature's antibiotic within the body. I also gave her 200 IU (International Units) of vitamin E and various B-complex vitamins and removed sugar, processed food products, and artificial coloring from her diet. Within one week, the number of her asthma attacks diminished.

Now we had to explore other stress factors. I asked the most important question you can ask such a child: "What is it that you wanted to say that you have never said?" I was asking Janine if she had been suppressing some feeling or thought. I wanted to know the cause of her asthma.

"Nothing," was her reply.

Janine's mother was in the room, so I brought her into the conversation. "Come on, Janine, I know there's something you wanted to say to your Mommy that you have been holding inside?"

"Nothing," she said again.

"All right. Then let's play a little game. I want you to close your eyes and get a picture of your Mommy in your mind. Now look at your Mommy closely in your mind. You can see her and you know there's something you want to tell her. What is it, Janine?"

"I . . . I wanted to say that I'm angry with you. I'm mad at you. I'm so mad. You don't cook nice foods. That's why I don't like you.

"And . . . and I don't like . . . I don't like what you do. You're never home for me. You love Daddy more than you love me. You love Chrissie (her sister) more than you love me." On and on went the torrents of anger she had accumulated. Each problem might have been minor by itself but, taken together, they had grown into a major problem whose only obvious sign was asthma.

We had to talk this through. I wanted her parents to handle this by themselves but they preferred working in my office with me mediating the conversations. They were hurt that she could have misperceived their love, yet they realized that they had to make some major changes if their daughter was to grow. They began working to reassure her and to improve communications as discussed earlier.

By the end of ten sessions, Janine was fine. Her asthma was gone and she felt closer to her parents.

Sometimes the problem your child suppresses can seem to have no solution. For example, one little boy came to me because of a nervous stomach for which the doctors could find no medical cause. When I asked him, "What is it that you wanted to say that you haven't said?" he responded, "I love you, Daddy, because Daddy never says I love you to me."

This was a rather sad and touching case. The child was ten years old and his father had left his mother. The man remarried, this time to a woman who had a six-year-old son. Then she got pregnant and soon there were two children. The father had neither the interest nor, in his own mind, the time for his first son. The child knew how much his mother was hurting so he suppressed his own feelings until they literally made him sick.

It would seem that in a case like this, nothing can be done. It would be better not to bring up the cause of the pain. The father was gone and apparently did not care about his child. The mother had enough problems without having the agony of hearing her son's grief when there was nothing she could do about it.

The child knows deep inside that some things will never change. The little boy knew that his father would not return. He knew that he could not influence anything by expressing his love for his father and his pain at the loss. Yet by saying his feelings aloud, he could get rid of them. Periodically he sat down with his mother to express his pain whenever the memories again overwhelmed him as they do for everyone. Once he verbalized his feelings anew, he was fine.

There is no subject too painful to discuss with your child. Talking may not be easy if the problem is one which has caused you hurt as well. However, talking is the one soothing balm which heals all old wounds. Suppression only causes the hurts of the past to fester and grow into mental and physical illness. Suppression can lead to fantastic distortions in your child's mind. Some children go so far as to create the misconception that a parent's divorce means that the parent died or now hates the child.

You can "save" a child's emotions by dealing with them honestly and openly. The travails of loss and rejection, if faced and discussed, can lead to increased emotional growth.

John was ten years old when he came to see me. He was moody at a time in life when most of his friends were in a more even emotional state. Some days he would feel good and other days he would feel depressed without reason.

I tried to get John to think more specifically about his moods. Many times a mood variation such as he was describing can come from undetected diet problems. One common cause of children's mood fluctuations is low blood sugar. The depressed state is caused by the blood sugar staying abnormally low because the adrenal glands' hormones, necessary to convert protein to sugar and fat, can't be produced.

"What did you have to eat before the days you felt depressed?"

"I don't know. It happens so much."

"What about the most recent time? Do you remember what was going on then?"

John thought for a moment, then said, "Yes, Daddy brought me a candy bar. He goes to the health food store and buys candy bars for me a lot. He brings me treats all the time."

"Do you have one with you now?" I asked. John did, and I read the ingredients listed on the label. As I suspected, the candy had a lot of sugar in it.

(Many people have misconceptions about health food stores. Such a store can be a source for both vitamins and numerous whole foods providing full nutrition. However, such stores are businesses and some of the products are offered simply because they sell.)

Perhaps the product label doesn't say sugar. The products may have corn syrup, dextrose, or some other ingredient which is just another term for processed sweetener. Once the sweetener reaches the bloodstream of someone with low blood sugar, it forces the glucose level in the blood to rise rapidly. Insulin is immediately triggered. This causes the glucose level to fall severely. Both extremes provide an abnormal roller-coaster reaction which results in overreactivity.

"Do your parents have diabetes?"

"Yes. Mom and Dad both have it. Grandfather does, too."

No one can say for certain, at this writing, that diabetes is hereditary, although a family predisposition is clear. Parents who eat sugary foods serve those same foods to their children. Since hypoglycemia, untreated, can develop into diabetes, the odds are in favor of a diabetic parent having a hypoglycemic child.

Suppose a mother loves to make rich, sugar-laden sweets, in addition to the regular meal. Even if the main dish, vegetable, salad, and other foods are good, well-balanced nutrition, the addition of the sweet dessert can throw the body out of balance.

I had John take the Seale-Harris test, a five-hour test showing how the body metabolizes sugar, and my suspicion of low blood sugar was correct. A hair analysis test handled by another doctor also showed that John was lacking in several minerals including chromium, another sign of a blood sugar problem.

John was placed on the basic diet discussed in this book. He was also provided with numerous vitamins such as pantothenic acid, vitamin B-6, and niacinamide.

The result of the diet change was that John stopped having extreme depression and was able to work more effectively in school.

Phyllis was nine years old and a total rebel. Discussions never took place at home. Instead, Phyllis screamed and her mother thought her daughter was overreacting to everything. Nothing was ever right and the child was filled with anger.

"Your parents tell me you've been feeling angry lately. What are you angry at?" I asked when Phyllis came to see me.

"I'm not angry," Phyllis screamed. "I'm not angry, so leave me alone!"

"You sound very angry to me," I said. "Who are you angry at?"

"Everybody! I hate everybody!"

"Who is everybody?" It is important to gently refine a child's thinking. There is a tendency to generalize when the real problem is quite specific.

"The whole stupid world. I don't like my teachers; I don't like my doctors. I don't like you, either. I don't like anybody."

Phyllis's parents told me that she was doing poorly in school and frequently failed to do her homework. Her mother tried to introduce vitamins but Phyllis refused to take them. She ate candy, though this did not seem to be the cause of her mood shifts. She did not seem to be having psychological problems from sugar metabolism.

"Let's try to take this a little slower so I can understand you better. Who are you angry at?"

"The whole world! Everybody!"

"I know that. But who, specifically? Your teachers?"

"Yes. I hate them."

"Why do you hate your teachers?"

"They're always siding with my mother."

"So you're actually more angry with your mother than you are with your teachers?"

"Yes. I'm angry at everybody."

"Who is everybody?"

Phyllis looked at me, a little frustrated with my probing. Then she said, "My parents."

"Which of your parents?"

"My mother."

"Why are you angry with your mother?"

"I'm angry because she had Stephen. Stephen's my baby brother. Why did she have to have Stephen? I was the only baby in the house. Everybody gave me all the attention and suddenly this little brat in diapers comes in and they pretend I don't exist anymore. They think they can only love one child at a time. They can't love two together, can they? That's what I'm angry about."

I encouraged Phyllis to keep talking. She needed to talk, to complain, to get out the anger.

If your child is very young when you begin applying the principles in this book, chances are that this kind of anger will not exist. However, if your child is older, there may be problems you unintentionally overlooked which have built up in your child. Most of us tend to focus on the immediate situations, without looking for the underlying cause. Once we get our children talking, though, it is important to act in a nonjudgmental manner and let them say everything that is affecting them.

I followed this approach with Phyllis. After she finished being angry, she started to cry, saying, "I really love my mother. It's just that she ignores me ever since the new baby came around."

"I suspect that your mother doesn't realize what she's doing," I told Phyllis. "Babies are so messy and troublesome that they need a lot of attention just to stay clean and out of trouble. You were like that when you were a baby but now you're so grown-up that you don't make a mess. I'll bet your mother is so happy with you that she forgot how much love you need to have to know you're good. If she knew you were unhappy I'll bet she'd show you how much she really cares and how happy she is to have you, especially since she has so much messy work with the new baby."

"I don't know. I don't think she cares."

"Would you like me to talk with her? Would you like me to tell her what you're feeling so we can both see if maybe she really does care?"

"She doesn't. I know it."

"She brought you to see me. If she wasn't worried about you, she never would have done that. I think you're pretty wonderful and maybe she does, too, or she wouldn't have brought you here. Why don't I talk with her and we'll see what happens?"

"Okay, but I don't know about this."

Of course you know what happened. The demands of the baby had been so great that Phyllis's mother never realized how her daughter was seeing the situation. As soon as I told Phyllis's mother what was happening, she reevaluated her actions and began spending extra time with her daughter. She gave her regular, devoted attention and Phyllis began to change. She stopped being angry because she again felt secure with her parents' love. Her schoolwork improved dramatically and she became a happy child again.

The more your child is willing to talk through the anger, the less of a problem it becomes. It is essential to express all the difficulties he or she is feeling in order for growth to take place. Thus you need to help your child refine the problem, from the general expression of anger to the specific details. Phyllis didn't hate the world, she was jealous of the attention given to her brother. It was necessary for her to be questioned concerning specifics before she could admit this, though.

Jimmy, an eleven-year-old, had a problem with sibling rivalry. He was not doing well in school and, when I got him to be specific, he finally said, "I just can't get along with my brother and sister. I'm unhappy because we fight all the time."

Children like Jimmy have to learn to face personal responsibility. They need to understand when a problem exists, they are a part of that problem. They have enough control to work for a solution and it is their responsibility to do so. However, to just say such an obvious fact could result in rebellion. It is better to ask questions which force the child to face his responsibility.

"Fighting with your brother and sister is your problem," I said. "Now how do you try to solve this problem."

Jimmy looked at me, slightly surprised. "I haven't, really," he said, surprised by his response.

"Then you haven't tried to solve your problem with your brother and sister?"

"No. I mean, I guess I try in a way. I tell them off when I'm upset."

"That hasn't worked, has it? It's hard to stop fighting by being angry and telling someone off, isn't it?"

"Yeah, it didn't work. Things just got worse."

"Have you tried to solve the problem any other way?"

I know that every answer Jimmy would give me would be a "nonsolution." He was always reacting to unpleasantness with more unpleasantness of his own. If somebody fought him, he would fight back. He hated the constant arguing but was making no effort to do anything else.

"I tried to fight with my brother and sister," said Jimmy. "That didn't stop it, so sometimes I get headaches. They just made it harder for me to get to sleep at night."

Jimmy sat, deep in thought for a minute, then began laughing. "You know, I've tried all those things to try and solve my problem but none of them worked. I guess I really never tried to handle my problem and I just told myself I was."

"Now you know that the ways you were using don't work. You can see that you weren't solving any problems. You were just keeping things bad. What could you have done that might really have worked?"

"I guess I could've sat down and talked with them. I've always gotten mad and fought them. I could just talk. Then we wouldn't be fighting."

"That seems like a good idea. Would it help you to bring them into my office? Would it be easier if you talked with them while I was sitting here?" This is a technique you can use, too. You can have your children come together for a talk while you act as both mediator and referee. Your presence reduces the chance of the talk becoming yet another fight. Jimmy understood this fact and agreed to have everyone come together in my presence.

The next day Jimmy returned with his younger sister and older brother. The children were close together in age, a situation which often increases the potential for sibling rivalry.

"Every kid fights with his brothers and sisters," said Jimmy's older brother, rather sullenly.

"I get the feeling that one of you really likes fighting with each other," I said. "And you're going to be living together for at least seven or eight more years. If you keep fighting, that time isn't going to be very much fun, and your home should be a place you enjoy. Maybe there's a way you three can get along together and have more fun. Why don't we talk about the reasons you fight and see if there might be some other ways to look at things."

"Jimmy keeps coming in and taking my things," said his older brother.

"Is that true?" I asked, and Jimmy admitted that sometimes he did take some of the things his brother had. "It's just for play. I always put them back."

"Everybody has possessions they think are special and they don't want anyone else to use," I said. "And everyone has things they like to share but they want to be asked first. They don't want somebody just taking them."

"Jimmy, I'll bet you have some things you don't want anybody touching unless you say it's okay, don't you?"

"I guess."

"So maybe one way to stop some of the fighting is to have a few rules all three of you can follow concerning your possessions. Why don't we decide that nobody takes anything from anybody else. If somebody wants to use something someone else has, you ask first. And if that person says 'no,' then that's the answer. It may not seem fair and you may know that person never used it, but you'll all agree to abide by whatever the other person says. Is that fair?"

"I guess. But I think my brother gets all bent out of shape for nothing" said Jimmy.

"Maybe you're right but you don't like the fighting, do you? With this rule, there's going to be less fighting, won't there?"

"Yeah, I suppose."

"Then maybe you three should adopt it."

"I guess. I mean, I guess I'd be mad if he took some of my things. He has more stuff, though. I mean . . . Well . . . Okay, I guess that will work. None of us will take the others' things unless we ask," said Jimmy.

"And if the person says 'no' you won't argue?"

"No. I guess that's fair."

"What about Jimmy always laughing at me?" said his sister. "He laughs at me when I tell him what I like on television. I tell him that I like the Muppets and he says that it's for kids. He makes fun of me and I don't like it."

"Is that true, Jimmy?"

"Yeah, I guess so."

"Okay, then this seems a good place for a second rule. You three have already agreed that you need your own space, that each of you should respect the other's possessions. Now I think you need to consider each other's opinions.

"Everybody has different opinions about what's enjoyable. That's why there are so many channels on television. If everybody liked the same things, there'd only be one channel and everybody would watch it.

"The fact that someone likes a particular television program, a particular book, or some activity doesn't make that person good or bad. That's just the way the person is and you'll find a whole lot of other people who share that opinion.

"Jimmy doesn't like the Muppet television show, and that's okay. A lot of adults like it and watch it all the time, but that doesn't make them dumb. You don't have to watch it if you don't want to, Jimmy, but I think that when you watch what you like, you should be allowed to do it without anyone making fun of you. Perhaps the next rule you three should have is that you will respect each other's opinions, even when they're different from your own. Does that seem fair?"

"You mean Jimmy can't make fun of my television shows anymore?"

"That's right, and you can't complain about what he watches. So long as you share, each taking turns watching whatever you like, the others can't complain. Does that seem fair?"

"Yeah, I guess," said Jimmy, the others also agreeing.

The session continued for half an hour. Each person had complaints about the other. It was not a case of Jimmy always being the villain, though he was brought to see me because he seemed to be having the most difficult time adjusting.

You, as a parent, can handle such problems the same way I did. Sit your children together and talk about what's wrong. Make certain that they all agree about the problems which exist. Then you decide the way they should handle the problem and present your solution as a suggestion.

Sometimes your child has a problem simply because he or she has never considered the alternate way to behave that is better for everyone. Take the case of Peter, a ten-year-old who was forever being ornery and difficult.

Peter had been seen by others and they had used approaches of which I heartily approve. One doctor placed Peter on vitamins to improve his behavior, yet nutrition was not the problem. His mother prepared excellent meals without sugar or processed food. She gave him vitamins and he took them willingly. Nothing happened.

Peter was told to meditate by another doctor. He refused, though neither that doctor nor I was convinced that it would make a difference. Something more was happening here and I was determined to find out what it was.

I talked with Peter a few minutes, then said, "Peter, we all know that there is a problem. I've heard from your mother and father. I've read what the other doctors have written. Now I'm turning to you. What do *you* think the problem is?"

"The problem is that I'm difficult," he said, both sheepishly and with a touch of pride.

"You're difficult? Being difficult is no fun. Everybody hassles you. Since you haven't stopped being difficult, I assume that you are doing something good that no one knows about. What problems has your being difficult solved? What reward do you get? How have you personally gained by being difficult?"

"I . . . I don't know what you mean."

"You're not going to be difficult unless you benefit. I'm just wondering what you get from acting like this."

"Wow," he said, embarrassed. He looked away, thinking. "I never thought . . ."

"What do you get?"

"I get . . . I get more attention, I guess. I'm difficult, so I get more attention than anybody else in the family. And I guess I get more sympathy. I get a lot of attention in school and . . . and I get more love because I'm difficult."

"Peter, I think you're telling me that you're being difficult deliberately. You don't really have a problem. You created this difficult person just to get attention."

"Yes, I think I did. But I didn't mean to do it, Dr. Green. I mean, I never sat down and thought that if I was difficult, I'd get more attention. I really never thought about it."

"I believe you, Peter. Many times we do things unconsciously and never think that we are doing it for a reason. Adults are like that, too. The important thing is that you have recognized why you did it. Since you know you created this, then you can stop it, too. You don't have to be difficult anymore because there really is no reason for it."

"What if there is?" said Peter, worried now that he had gained this insight into himself. "If I'm not difficult anymore, will my parents still love me? They seem to love me more when I'm difficult than when I'm not difficult."

"I'm going to talk with them about that, but I don't think there's going to be a problem. Love never stops with a parent. Your Mommy and Daddy will always love you no matter how you act. However, there's a difference between getting attention and having a happy relationship.

"I'll bet that when you're difficult, your parents are a little frustrated with you, aren't they? I'll bet they're a little annoyed and none of you are really enjoying each other's company right at that moment. You're getting attention but it's the wrong kind.

"When you're not difficult, I'll bet that you all have much more fun. I'll bet you find yourself sharing with them and doing things together that make all of you much happier. I'll talk with your parents and then you can all try and see. Is that all right with you?"

"That makes sense. I'll give it a try."

Naturally, what I said was in Peter's best interest. The family enjoyed each other more. Although Peter had previously had few friends, he became extremely popular and his grades improved.

This situation has occurred with other children. One little girl, nine-year-old Beatrice, was always depressed. Her diet was changed, she learned meditation, she exercised, but nothing stopped the depression. She had had tests to see if she was ill or had physical problems, but the tests all showed that nothing was wrong. Finally she was brought to see me.

"I think it's time we were honest with each other. You're always depressed and there's absolutely no reason for you to be so sad. All the usual problems which might cause depression apparently don't exist with you. I have to assume that you're making yourself depressed because you're getting something out of it. What's the payoff?"

Beatrice stared at me, her eyes so wide I thought she was going into shock. Then she burst out laughing and said, "You weren't supposed to ask me that. No one's ever asked me that." I knew I had hit something important.

"I *did* ask and I want to know what you get out of it?"

"I get Mommy to love me. I get Daddy to love me. And . . ."

Suddenly Beatrice understood herself in a way she had never considered. She knew that she was manipulating her family by acting depressed. She also knew that it was not the best way to behave. However, until she actually verbalized what she was doing, she never realized how foolish this was.

As with Peter, the discovery did not mean instant change. She had a natural fear that any change in her behavior would mean a loss of love. However, as with Peter, I was able to work with her and with her parents so that she continued to see that she received the love she craved without having to create the appearance of depression.

It is easy to focus on just one aspect of what is happening with your child and miss the underlying cause. By talking with your children and following the techniques used in the examples in this chapter, you will find that you can quickly and easily overcome difficulties.

All children want to feel happy, loved, and good about themselves. When you provide positive support, eliminating the misguided notions which come from their limited experience in life, you help increase their ability to reach their tremendous potential. You will bring forth the exceptional traits that are so important for a full life.

10

Conclusion

By now you understand that having an exceptional child is not a matter of heredity so much as it is a combination of love, close interaction, positive encouragement and sensitivity to each child's individuality. It is accepted that most people never tap more than a small percentage of their brain power; we seldom attempt to find the limits of our potential. Children can have unresolved fears, fantasies, and self-doubts which can prevent them from trying.

Heredity might be a determinant in the potential of the human mind, but your love and guidance will be the ultimate determinant. A baby cannot freely explore the world around him without constantly knowing that his parents love him and that he is safe. The baby who fails to explore is a baby who cannot learn and grow. Without unfettered growth exceptional quality can't develop.

A child who goes to school may feel picked on by teachers and classmates. A loving hug, the total acceptance of a parent, and an adult ear for his problems will give that child the strength to try again. A child must know that a parent has consistent and unconditional approval of all positive actions. With this loving support, your child will meet each growth phase as a new challenge. Without this support, your child may shrink back from developing properly.

A child whose life is planned, organized by others, compartmentalized, and made into a stifling routine will rebel. Sometimes this means doing nothing, playing the "fool," and appearing to be of limited ability. Other times this means doing exactly the opposite of what adults may desire. Yet even this recalcitrance is your child's effort at growth.

Nutrition and exercise are crucial building blocks for your child's development. Improper sugar metabolism can cause hyperactivity preventing concentration and producing anxiety and depression. A diet rich in foods such as those mentioned in the appendix will help your child focus his or her full mind and energies on learning.

Exercise in the sunlight is important for the same reason. Exercise keeps children healthy, fit, and their brain well oxygenated. Many foods rich in the B-complex vitamins act as natural calmatives. This is especially true with pantothenic acid and niacinamide.

Meditation allows a child to relax, to learn to concentrate, and to be focussed and quiet—all skills essential to being able to learn in school.

Visualization helps a child mobilize personal goals. It is a technique which allows for both change and self-understanding leading to change. It is also a way for you and your child to communicate more effectively.

Experimentation through music and art allows parents to communicate with each child's unique expression—the actualization of the child's creative potential.

Exercises that give your child an understanding of the feelings of others through the methods described enable your child to grow to be sympathetic to others, loving, accepting of faults and to become a more mature, likable person. Use your understanding and the methods described in the preceding chapters as tools to nurture a creative child who will develop into an exceptional adult.

You are increasing loving interaction. This will enhance the lives of you and your child, bringing you both many years of happiness.

APPENDIX

Many parents worry about trying to change their children's diets. They see how much their children love fast-food hamburgers and don't want to deprive them of the pleasure. What they fail to realize is that a healthful diet does not have to be a rigid, "no fun" diet. Perhaps the fast-food hamburger has to be abandoned because the cheese is heavily processed, the bun has white flour and sugar, and there are other additives making it of low nutritional value (more nutrients are needed for metabolization than are supplied by the meal). However, you can make the same hamburger using whole cheese, a whole wheat bun without sugar, and similar ingredients which will look and taste nearly identical.

The same situation is true with desserts. Brownies can be made with the natural food carob and honey instead of sugar.

Most health food stores sell a variety of cookbooks. These usually emphasize dishes with whole grains, fresh vegetables, and fruits. The recipes generally require neither processed ingredients nor sugar.

The following foods are listed as a general guide. They are all foods which offer no stress to the system and can be included in your menu plans. The list is a suggestion, not a guide to be rigidly followed. Other foods can be consumed if you follow the precautions shown in the chapter on nutrition. This list is just meant to help you as you begin planning the physical development of your exceptional child.

Meat, Fish, Fowl: Fish and poultry are generally better for your child than beef but beef is good. It should be lean, and if you can introduce organ meats—liver, heart, etc.—to the diet, they are of high nutritional value. Foods such as oysters, salmon, and eggs are all rich in vitamin B-12 which provides the type of energy needed for learning.

Vegetables: These are probably dirty words for your children but all children love some vegetables and the list is long. Among the good ones are asparagus, avocado, beets, broccoli, brussels sprouts, cabbage, carrots, cauliflower, celery, cucumber, eggplant, green beans, lettuce, lima beans, onions, radishes, sauerkraut, squash, string beans, tomatoes, turnips, and zucchini.

Fruits: Among the best fruits are apricots, berries, grapefruit, melons, oranges, peaches, pears, pineapples, and tangerines. These are good both raw and cooked. Apples, for example, can be baked without sugar and still make a sweet dessert. Naturally, cream and sugar should not be included, but milk can. Canned fruit is good only when purchased in the water pack. Make certain the label says no sugar added. All fruit sold in syrup pack has been heavily sugared.

Juices: Any unsweetened fruit or vegetable juice is good for your children. Be certain to read the label and avoid fruit drinks which are only partially fruit, "ades" which are high in sugar, and other sweet beverages.

Desserts: Ideally you will avoid sweets, though desserts made with all natural products are fine. Avoid pies, cake, candy, and any other sugared products. Encourage the eating of fresh fruit, nuts, seeds, soybeans for dessert, and cheese.

Baked potatoes with the full skin are excellent for children. Brown rice (it looks off-white, not brown, despite the name) is unprocessed as is bulgur wheat and buckwheat groats. Processed mashed potatoes without the skin and similarly prepared products are nutritionally deficient.

Bread should be whole wheat or rye. Read the ingredients of commercial products. Some without sugar or preservatives are available in regular supermarkets. Others, with similar sounding names, do have such problem additives.

There are certain foods which are natural calmatives. These include whole milk, soy milk, fish, beef, soy flour, organ meats, shellfish, and eggs. Magnesium, important for your child, is in whole wheat, soy flour, oatmeal, peas, brown rice, whole corn, beans, and nuts.

BIBLIOGRAPHY

BECK, JOAN. *How to Raise a Brighter Child.* New York: Trident Press, 1967.
BENSON, HERBERT. *Relaxation Response.* New York: Morrow, 1975.
BRODY, JANE. "From Fertility to Mood, Sunlight Found to Affect Human Biology," *New York Times,* June 23, 1981.
DAVIS, ADELLE. *Let's Have Healthy Children.* New York: Harcourt Brace Jovanovich, 1951.
———. *Let's Eat Right to Keep Fit.* New York: Harcourt Brace Jovanovich, 1954.
DODSON, FITZGERALD. *How to Parent.* Los Angeles: Nash, 1970.
ENGELMAN, SIEGFRIED, and THERESE ENGELMAN. *Give Your Child a Superior Mind.* New York: Simon and Schuster, 1966.
ERIKSON, ERIK H. *Childhood and Society.* New York: Norton, 1963.
FRAIBERG, SELMA H. *The Magic Years.* New York: Scribner's, 1959.
GINOTT, HAIM G. *Between Parent and Child.* New York: Macmillan, 1965.
GREEN, ELMER, and ALYCE GREEN. *Beyond Biofeedback.* New York: Delacorte/Seymour Lawrence, 1977.
HUIZINGA, JOHN. *Homo Ludens.* Boston: Beacon, 1972.
ILG, L. FRANCES, and LOUISE AMES BATES. *Gesell Book of Child Behavior.* New York: Harper, 1955.
ILLICH, IVAN. *Medical Nemesis.* New York: Pantheon, 1976.
KHAN, PIR VILAYAT INAYAT. *Toward the One.* New York: Harper Colophon, 1974.

———. *Samadhi with Open Eyes*. New Lebanon, N.Y.: Sufi Order Publication, 1978.

———. *The Message of Our Time*. New York: Harper & Row, 1979.

KOESTLER, ARTHUR. *Act of Creation*. New York: Macmillan, 1964.

MASLOW, A.H. *The Farther Reaches of Human Nature*. New York: Viking, 1971.

MASTERS, ROBERT, and JEAN HOUSTON. *Mind Games*. New York: Viking, 1972.

MONTAGU, ASHLEY. *Touching*. New York: Columbia University Press, 1971.

ORNSTEIN, ROBERT E. *The Psychology of Consciousness*. San Francisco: W.H. Freeman, 1972.

OTT, JOHN. *Health and Light*. Old Greenwich, Conn.: Devin Adair, 1973.

PEARSE, JOSEPH CHILTON. *The Crack in the Cosmic Egg*. New York: Julian Press, 1971.

PIAGET, JEAN. *The Moral Judgement of the Child*. New York: The Free Press/Macmillan, 1965.

ROZMAN, DEBORAH. *Meditating with Children*. Boulder Creek, Calif.: University of the Trees Press, 1975.

———. *Meditation for Children*. Boulder Creek, Calif.: University of the Trees Press, 1976.

SCHRAG, PETER and DIANE DIVOKY. *The Myth of the Hyperactive Child*. New York: Pantheon, 1975.

SIMEONS, A.T.W. *Man's Presumptuous Brain*. New York: Dutton, 1962.

SMITH, LENDON. *Feed Your Kids Right*. New York: McGraw-Hill, 1979.

SULLIVAN, WALTER. "The Einstein Papers: A Flash of Insight Came After Long Reflection on Relativity," *New York Times*, March 28, 1972.

WEBB, WILSE B. *Sleep, the Gentle Tyrant*. Englewood Cliffs, N.J.: Spectrum Book/Prentice Hall, 1975.

WEISBERGER, ELEANOR. *Your Young Child and You*. New York: Dutton, 1975.

INDEX

Alpha waves, 56, 79–80
Altruism, 87–89
   meditation techniques and, 92–93
Anger, 153–56
   expression of, 109–11
   yelling as expression of, 102–3
Antibiotics, 39
Artwork
   communication and, 107–9
   See also Drawing
Asthma, 150–51
Attention
   bedtime requests for, 138–39
   being difficult as way of getting, 160–61
   meditation and focusing of, 76–77
Auditory stimulation, 12

Babbling, 10
Bates, Louise Ames, 19, 32
B-complex vitamins, 34–35, 37–40
Bedroom, parents', 140
Bedtime
   crying at, 137, 139
   fears at, 141
   "just one more" syndrome at, 138
   music at, 136
   rituals for, 138, 139
   security and reassurance at, 135–37
   talking to your child at, 136–37
   three- and four-year-olds at, 139–41
   two-year-olds at, 137–39
Bedwetting, 143
Beta waves, 79
Biotin, 39
Blood sugar, low, 152–54
Boredom, 62, 63
Brain waves
   meditation and, 55–56, 79–80
   during sleep, 133–34
Breakfast, 35, 37
Breast feeding, 34
Breathing, meditation and, 77–78
Brody, Jane, 38

Calcium, 42
Caring for others, 91–95, 98

Child-proofing, 46
Choline, 34, 40
Communication, 99–131
  anger and, 153–56
  artwork and, 107–9
  play and, 103–6
  projection and, 105–8
  sibling rivalry and, 155–59
  suppression of problems and, 151–52
  of thoughts and feelings, 109–11
  visualization techniques and, 113–31
  yelling and, 101–3
Compassion, 87–88
Copper, 44
"Copy cat" game, 5
Creativity, 107
  alpha waves and, 79–80
  child's understanding of, 54, 55
Crying at bedtime, 137, 139
Curiosity, 3–5, 46

Daydreaming, 74, 117–18
Delta waves, 79
Depression, 152–53, 161–62
Desserts, 166
Development, 7–32
  of five- and six-year-olds, 22–23
  of four-year-olds, 17–18
  intellectual, 29–30
  myths about, 2
  of nine-year-olds, 25
  of obedience to parents, 31–32
  of one-year-olds, 7–13
  of seven- to eight-year-olds, 23
  of sibling relationships, 30–31
  of ten-year-olds, 27–28
  tests of, *see* Tests
  of two-year-olds, 13–15
  of three-year-olds, 15–17

Diabetes, 153
Diet, 62, 165–67
  mood fluctuations and, 152–54
  planning your child's, 36–37
  schizophrenia and, 147
  See also Nutrition
Discipline, 45–49
  See also Punishment
Dolomite, 42, 142
"Dot" exercise, 74
Drawing, 21, 54, 107–8
  fantasizing about, 56–57
Dreams, 141

Einstein, Albert, 13, 71–72
Empathy, 91–93
Environment
  exploring the, 46–47
  for meditation, 75
Exercise, 164
Exploration, 46–47, 112
  painting and drawing as, 107

Fairy tales, 52–53
Fantasy, 49–50, 74
Fantasy games, 51–69
  hiding a stuffed toy, 54
  "peace," 51–52
  peek-a-boo, 53–54
  for school-age children, 58–59
  visualization techniques and, 56–61
Fatty acids, 41
Fats, hydrogenated, 37
Fears, 28–29
  at bedtime, 141
Feelings
  expression of, 109–11
  See also Anger
Fetus, meditation and, 72

Fish, 165–66
Flour, white, 35–36
Folic acid, 39
Fractional relaxation, 56, 59–61, 92
Friend, imaginary, 49–50
Fruits, 166

Games
 "copy cat," 5
 word, 68–69
 See also Fantasy games
Giving, 87–88, 98
Grades, 120–21

Hiding a stuffed toy, 54
Hydrogenated fats, 37
Hyperactivity, 148–50
Hypersomnia, 144–45
Hypoglycemia, 152–54

Ilg, Frances, 19, 32
Illnesses, 28
Illogic, 50
Imaginary friend, 49–50
Imagination
 of four-year-olds, 18–19
 See also Fantasy
Independence, 100–1
Inositol, 39
Insomnia, 146
Intellectual curiosity, *see* Curiosity
Intellectual development, phases of, 29–30
Intuition, 71–72
Iron, 43

Journal, keeping a, 5

Juices, 166
"Just one more" syndrome at bedtime, 138

Language development
 of one-year-olds, 10–13
 of three-year-olds, 17
Latchkey program, 100
Lecithin, 40
Lighting, 38
Logic, 50
Love, 163
 increasing a child's capacity for, 93–94
 as reinforcement, 111–12
Low blood sugar, 152–54

Magnesium, 42–43, 167
Manganese, 43
Meditation, 55–58, 71–85, 164
 altruism and, 92–93
 benefits of, 71
 breathing and, 77–78
 comfortable position for, 75
 creativity and, 79–80
 daydreaming and fantasy distinguished from, 74–75
 "dot" exercise, 74
 environment for, 75
 focusing the child's attention and, 76–77
 getting your child into, 75–76
 idea, concept, or object to dwell on during, 75
 passive attitude and, 75
 relaxation and, 78–79, 81
 schedule for, 75
 visualization and, 80–84
 "wave" exercise, 72–73
Math, fantasy games and, 58–61

Milk
    mother's, 34
    warm, as sleeping medication, 142
Minerals, 42–44
Mood fluctuations, 152–54
Motor skills (mobility), 9–10
Music, 12
    at bedtime, 136
Musical instruments, 54–55

Napping, 142–43
Night-lights, 141
Nightmares, 141
"No," saying, 46–47
Nocturnal wanderings, 139, 140
Nursing, 34
Nutrition, 33–44, 164–67
    See also Diet; *and specific nutrients*

Obeying parents, changes in attitude toward, 31–32
Ott, John, 38

PABA (para-amino benzoic acid), 39
Painting, 107–8
Pantothenic acid, 35, 39
"Peace" game, 51–52
Peek-a-boo, 53–54
Play
    communication and, 103–6
    See also Games
Positive reinforcement, 53, 59
Poultry, 165–66
Praise, as reinforcement, 111–12
Projection, 105–8
Protein, in mother's milk, 34

Punishment, 88–92
Psychosynthesis, 65
Puzzles, 4–5

Quality of time spent with your child, 3

Reading aloud
    fairy tales, 53
    stories, 5, 21
Relaxation
    fractional, 56, 59–61, 92
    meditation and, 78–79, 81
    See also Meditation
REM (rapid eye movement) sleep, 134–35
Ritalin, 3–4
Rituals, bedtime, 138, 139
Rocking your baby, 136

Schizophrenia, childhood, 147
Scribbling, 15
Seale-Harris test, 153,
Sensory stimulation, 10
Sexual relations, seeing, 140
Sharing, 16–17, 90–91
Sibling relationship, at different ages, 30–31
Sibling rivalry, 145, 155–59
Sleep, 8–9, 133–46
    age and variations in patterns of, 141
    amount of, 141
    excessive, 144–45
    problems with, 141–46
    REM (rapid eye movement), 134–35
    See also Bedtime; Insomnia; Napping

Sleeping medications, 141–42
Sodium, 43
Speech, see Language development
Stories, reading, 5, 21
Stress, vitamin C and, 40–41
Stress-related problems, 150
Sugar, 34–36
   mood fluctuations and, 152–54
Sunlight, vitamin D obtained from, 38
Suppression of problems, 151–52

Talking to your child, 10–12
   at bedtime, 136–37
Teachers, parents as, 2
Television, 38, 94–97
   four-year-olds and, 19–20
   insomnia and, 146
Tests
   for one-year-olds, 7–9
   for two-year-olds, 13–14
   for three-year-olds, 15–16
   for five- and six-year-olds, 21–22
   for seven- to eight-year-olds, 24–25
   for nine- to ten-year-olds, 26–27
Theta waves, 56, 80
Toys, sharing, 90–91
Trace minerals, 44

Vegetables, 166
Verbal development, see Language development
Violence, television and, 94–97
Visualization techniques, 56–61, 72, 164
   meditation and, 80
Visual stimulation, 12
   communication and, 113–31
Vitamin A, 38
Vitamin B-complex, 34–35, 37–40
Vitamin B-1, 34
Vitamin B-3, 35
Vitamin B-6, 35
Vitamin B-12, 35
Vitamin C, 40–41, 150
Vitamin D, 38
Vitamin E, 41
Vitamin K, 41
Vitamin supplements, 38
Vitamins, 37–43
   fat-soluble, 37–38
   water-soluble, 37
"Wave" exercise, 72–73
Word games, 68–69

Yelling at your child, 101–3

Zinc, 34, 43